ADVANCE

"There has been a great deal written about organizational change, but if there is anyone who can contribute new thinking to this subject, it is Neil Usher. Neil's new book takes a practical look at change – busting the myths and setting out just what needs to be done to make change successful. It's astonishingly well written in Neil's unique and engaging style. If you do change stuff, you should read this book. In the current context, it could not be a more timely read."

Gem Dale
Lecturer, Liverpool John Moores University

"I love the conversational style of *Elemental Change*, the personal references, the human language, the exercises, and the references to previous points in Neil's career. It's exudes confidence and credibility and is a very authentic read."

Natasha Wallace
Founder and chief coach, Conscious Works
and author of *The Conscious Effect*

"Finally we can ditch all those business books on change that give you numerous theories and models and not a lot of reality. Here's the common-sense approach from Neil; been there, done it, some of it worked and some didn't, here's what to avoid. All with a side helping of humour. (To be honest, I was hooked at the first mention of Viz!)"

Liz Kentish
Co-founder, Kentish and Co.

"*Elemental Change* is your chance to defy the dismal stats of change management failure by understanding what's really at the elemental heart of organizational shape-shifting. Neil is expert and erudite. He provokes us to ponder while sharing his practical advice. A winning combination."

Shawn Callahan
Founder, Anecdote International and
author of *Putting Stories to Work*

"This human, accessible and amusing book metaphorically speaks to you where you're at, in ways that connect to you. Using simple, effective frameworks and tools it brings concepts to life through experience."

Dr Anne Marie Rattray
Founder, The Skills Space and author of
Smart Working: Creating the Next Wave

"A book to push under the nose of anyone who says that people hate change. Neil reminds us that change isn't 'a thing' – it's part of us, and it's perpetual. The nature of life is change and it only hurts when we don't get the change we want. The book provides a range of tools, stories and anecdotes written for anyone who is involved with changing organizations. Which is all of us."

Paul Taylor
Innovation Coach, Bromford Lab

"This book is packed full of advice for managing change in an empathic way. It has systems to follow, tips for unsticking people and lots of explanation on why change can be so difficult for some. Things are always easier to deal with if you know why it's happening in the first place. If you have change on the horizon and need the knowledge and confidence to deal with it in a way that gets everyone working together, get your hands on a copy of this book. It includes humour too – always a good thing."

Julie Brown
Business and PR coach

"Successful change means figuring out not just *what* to do, but also what's *worth* doing. Aristotle called this 'phronesis': practical wisdom. In *Elemental Change*, Neil draws on a career's worth of phronesis to explore the key to any change initiative: what *should* be done, with a cracking set of thinking tools to help!"

Ian Ellison
Co-founder, 3edges and podcast host of Workplace Matters

"Neil Usher has produced a wide-ranging and inspiring guide to building organizational change when things don't stand still. In fact, very little stands still, but it's taken until now for people like Neil to realize this and really move the organizational change dial from fighting instability to embracing it and making it a central plank of change-making for the 21st century. With the signature Elemental framework, punchy writing style and years of experience, this book is an important part of a new movement in organizational transformation."

Mark McKergow
International speaker, consultant and author of *The Solutions Focus, Host: Six New Roles of Engagement for Teams, Organizations, Communities, Movements* and *Hosting Generative Change*

"Even though I've been working in change management for the past 20 years, this book really makes me think and gives me new perspectives. It is like a kind of out of body experience!"

Kati Barklund
Senior Workplace Strategy Manager

Published by
LID Publishing Limited
The Record Hall, Studio 304,
16-16a Baldwins Gardens,
London EC1N 7RJ, UK

info@lidpublishing.com
www.lidpublishing.com

A member of:

businesspublishersroundtable.com

Printed by Gutenberg Press, Malta
ISBN: 978-1-912555-85-7
ISBN: 978-1-911671-19-0 (ebook)

Cover illustration: Simon Heath and Matthew Renaudin
Page design: Caroline Li

NEIL USHER

ELEMENTAL CHANGE

MAKING STUFF HAPPEN WHEN
NOTHING STANDS STILL

MADRID | MEXICO CITY | LONDON
NEW YORK | BUENOS AIRES
BOGOTA | SHANGHAI | NEW DELHI

CONTENTS

HAT TIPS

With massive thanks to the following for an absolutely vital mix of advice, insight, encouragement and refreshingly honest feedback at various stages of the marathon: Kati Barklund, Julie Brown, Antony Byrne, Shawn Callahan, Mark Catchlove, Tom Cheesewright, Gem Dale, Bruce Davison, Khurshed Dehnugara, Chris Dinning, David D'Souza, Ian Ellison, Mark Eltringham, Kursty Groves, Lance Hamilton-Griffiths, Giverny Harman, Chris Kane, Liz Kentish, Mark McKergow, Dr Nigel Oseland, Gill Parker, Polly Plunket-Checkemian, Ros Pomeroy, Dr Anne Marie Rattray, Silvia Rivela, Doug Shaw, Pallavi Shrivastava, Paul Taylor, Perry Timms, Natasha Wallace and Sandy Wilkie.

Extra special thanks go to the incredibly brilliant Ana Neves and Fiona Tribe who, in reviewing and commenting on the draft, made me look deeper into my thinking and ideas than I thought possible. If you ever meet, I'd like to be there.

Sincere gratitude to all the super folk at LID including Aiyana, Susan, Francesca, Caroline, Osaro, Matthew, Niki and Martin, and to Sue for a marvellous copy edit.

To Kate, Ava and Mae for love, encouragement, patience and fun. Always. And forever.

This book is dedicated to the memory of my most excellent friend Paul. Taken far too early, always with me. Love you, mate.

FOREWORD

BY

KHURSHED DEHNUGARA

We walk into a new section of the building. My footfall is definitely less heavy, something has changed in the thickness of the floor covering. It is quiet here, too, as if we have closed the door on the real world of this business and entered hallowed ground.

The two people we are here to meet are immaculately dressed, the clothing is all very 'on-trend' and I feel slightly intimidated, the way I do when entering a luxury retail store. They are leading the CEO's strategy group, a team of change agents responsible for directing key transformational activities across the organization. As far as I understand, it is a kind of skunkworks set up to handle strategic innovation and we are talking to them because they are a little stuck.

Their smiles are cold, and we begin with a time check. We have 60 minutes, but they need to be away in 45, important business for the CEO. It's always for the CEO. There are regular time checks every ten minutes from one or the other monitoring our progress, and I'm more than a little pissed off before the second one.

There is no space to breathe here.

They hand-select high-potential individuals from the global business and bring them to the corporate headquarters for a 12-month stint. They are tasked with making a breakthrough on some issue of strategy that a local business unit has dragged its heels on. After doing the 'thinking,' they hand it back to the business unit and, hopefully, as a result of their increased profile and access to the CEO, go on to an immediate promotion back home. There doesn't seem to be a downside. Not for them, anyway.

The team was run by the two people I was meeting: one was the leader, the other an internal process consultant with a specialism in Six Sigma–type approaches, but they don't call them that any more. They coached the selected few during their time in the corporate headquarters. As I was already experiencing, there was a significant emphasis on process and structure and being neat, ordered, smart.

The problem was, they were having no breakthroughs. Even those they claimed to have had looked good on paper but didn't stand up to much scrutiny. Few changes were sustained, partly because *the local business resented being given an answer to implement, partly because there was no space for creativity, diversity, disturbance or difference. And it all showed up in the conversation. I call it a conversation, but it was more of an examination. They were looking for quick, easy answers and weren't too keen on a world view that challenged their own highly developed perception. We were in the way.*

Most of all, there was no room for anything outside of their prescribed process. As we were escorted back over the perimeter, I noticed my chest expand a little and let out a couple of deep sighs before I felt 'back in my body' again. You won't be surprised to hear this was another of my not-so-glorious failures and we weren't invited back for another conversation.

As I recount this story, I realize that people like Neil and I have been having this experience for the whole of our careers, several decades in the making. We are in an ongoing fight for the soul of our corporations. Trying to wrestle it away from those that would sit on new ideas in favour of 'safety,' cost-cutting and inconsequential incremental improvements, from those that would use control processes and personal incentives to actively discourage people from making any meaningful change and from those that would rather protect their own career than safeguard the organization and people they're responsible for.

When I look at this population with a compassionate eye, I wonder if they're simply lacking an understanding of the ancient philosophies and modern practices that underpin today's successful change agency. In the absence of this education maybe a reversion to security and control is all that's available. Maybe change is another task to close off rather than an exciting adventure to be experienced. That's where this book makes its contribution.

As Neil says in the chapter 'Universal thinking,' "change isn't something to fear – it's our essence. We're predisposed toward it. We mustn't defeat ourselves before we've begun."

Neil brings just enough philosophy, just enough academic research and just enough practical experience to this writing. He weaves all three together into a clear structure with a sharp, funny, storytelling style that gives the writing a compelling, engaging momentum. This isn't a book to strike the fear of change into you, as many often do. It is a book that encourages you to see the opportunities and want to get on with it, to challenge – and to see everything else changing around you as revealing gaps, not erecting barriers. I know his energy and writing will be a substantial contribution to the field.

Khurshed Dehnugara
Author of *The Challenger Spirit: Organizations that Disturb the Status Quo* (2011), *Flawed but Willing: Leading Large Organizations in the Age of Connection* (2014) and *100 Mindsets of Challenger Leaders* (2019).

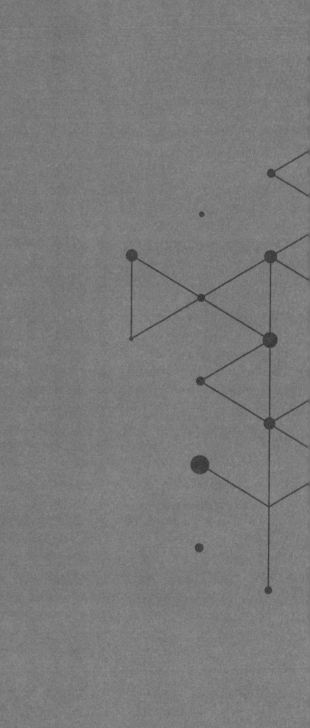

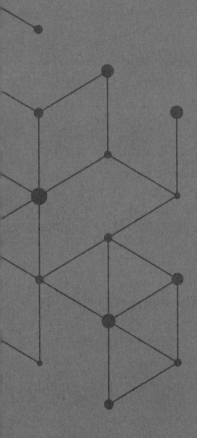

OPENING
GAMBIT

CHANGE REALITIES ...

Open, prepared, dextrous, resourceful and optimistic. The right mindset is vital in leading a change initiative, quite as much as anything practical we can do. It can be shocked, cajoled or encouraged. We'll opt for the last of the three with a little orientation and a few teasers for starters. We'll explore these provocations in more depth throughout the rest of the book.

Why start here? You're likely to have picked this book up after your change initiative has already begun, and you're in it up to a given part of your anatomy. The conveyor belt has started and its mechanical shimmy is inducing a mild nausea. Everyone's looking to you, and you're not sure where to look. The floor, popular as it seems to be at times like this, is overrated. The guiding star you think you've seen is a communication satellite signalling it's time to sort it out.

So, we'll sort it out together.

CHANGE ISN'T A THING

Change doesn't exist as a 'thing' in its own right. We believe we can define, measure and manage it. If we can give it a persona, we can ascribe qualities to it like 'easy' or 'difficult.' Yet while we can see it happening, noticing that things aren't the same as they were, we can't actually *see* it. We can say there has been a change, something is changing, or it needs to change, but not "Oh look, there's change." We can say it's chaotic, beguiling, intriguing but in doing so we're portraying the process rather than ascribing characteristics in the abstract. They're always the properties of a distinctive instance, the thing or situation that's changing.

WE CAN'T STEP OUTSIDE CHANGE – BUT WE CAN LEAD IT FROM WITHIN

When leading change, we can't abstract our self from it. Somewhere, our own life – our career, relationships or reputation – will be tangled up with what we've been asked to do, and so we're within the story. Due to the interconnectedness of all things, we're inherently conflicted. But so is everyone. We instinctively regard 'conflicted' as a negative, but it's simply a reality. As we'll discover, that's a bucket full of opportunities and the very same bucket full of problems.

WE CAN'T MASTER CHANGE – BUT WE CAN LEARN TO WORK WITH IT

While larger organizations sometimes acquire a specialist 'change' function, most of the time as managers and leaders we're expected to understand and complete an initiative ourselves. Every circumstance we encounter will be unique. We may have developed a knack for leading change, but whether tackling a similar situation in a different organization or a different challenge in the same organization, a part of us will always be a novice. In each situation we'll need to draw on our experience, resources, connections, organizational skills and simple sense in differing degrees in working with change.

WE CAN'T DEFINE A START OR END TO CHANGE – BUT WE CAN CREATE HELPFUL BOUNDARIES

As of today, our change initiative has already started. In fact, it did so long before we thought it had and will go on far longer than we think it will. We're joining too late and we'll leave too early. Change initiatives begin with the flicker of an idea that emerges from the rearrangement of other thoughts, related and not. It's often unconscious before we're able to form it. When the initiative is substantially complete in its recognizable form, it splits like a delta, breaking down into a multitude of smaller paths. Each is related but with a character of its own, and an inherent potential for growth. Yet we top and tail it, as we need to feel as though it's begun and ended. We use events or dates to which we can relate. As we'll see, leading change invites a myriad of conveniences.

CHANGE SUCCESS IS HIGHLY POSSIBLE
– BUT RARELY ABSOLUTE

Apart from the Ancient Greeks, as will become apparent, one of my early and entirely unlikely change heroes was Professor Piehead from the UK's satirical *Viz Comic*. He would always happily proclaim, after blowing up himself (and his lab assistant Tim, who he always calls Joe) in a preposterous experiment: "Yet another partial success!" His optimism was irrepressible, and he understood that change succeeds by degree, not in the absolute. Quite probably, accidentally.

CHANGE CAN BE OURS TO GUIDE
– BUT IT'S NOT EXCLUSIVE

We're trying to get things done but all around us everything is constantly shifting. We don't have control of the whole train set. Others want to play – and they do, yet we didn't invite them. Our train set overlaps with other train sets. Our trains are suddenly on another track, and other trains are on ours. New trains form from theirs and ours. We're not always sure where the trains are heading. From time to time one crashes. No one seems to be in charge. What seemed like a closed system is revealed to be part of a seemingly infinite one. We must learn to share the train set and be open to its limitless scale. As a child, sharing was one of our earliest lessons and possibly the one that has taken the longest to land. If it's landed at all.

... AND MYTHS

Just as there are provocations containing both a challenge and a way forward, there are inevitably myths that need dispelling. There are four principal offenders we need to discharge at this stage, or at least cast into enough doubt to create confidence. There will be others along the way.

WE HATE CHANGE

Whenever I hear the expression "people hate change," a little part of me dies. It's an all-encompassing generalization that helps to prepare for, or to post-rationalize, failure. It posits inherently impossible odds. In attempting to illuminate everything, it explains nothing. It's as absurd as saying we dislike weather. As we'll unpack in more detail in Part One, hating change means we'd rather not be here at all. That can't be discounted, of course. Yet without our innate, unquenchable thirst for change, collectively and individually, our ancestors probably wouldn't have got much further than the end of the Olduvai Gorge. That's not to say that opposition to specific changes may not arise, but that's an entirely different proposition to an instinctive rejection of *all* change. It's the most baseless, unhelpful and distracting myth we have to dispel in leading change. We'll give it our best shot.

THE PACE OF CHANGE IS INCREASING

And there's nothing we can do to stop or slow it. It's become a fashionable idea in commercial circles and there are some excellent books about it.[1] While it may be the case with some things, and we may be able to cite evidence, it can't be proven universally. We often perceive only surface-level change, noisy rather than significant, and not that which lies deeper. We often see technological advancement as an illustration of accelerating change, yet there are coherent arguments that the pace of innovation has actually slowed.[2] Taking the view that change is getting faster leaves us with a sense that we're being left behind, that there's nothing we can do to stay the course.

We feel our energy dissipating and are about to give up, just at the point we're ready to begin. In which case we wouldn't feel up to facing anything at all. Yet this doesn't happen. Our resources have remained a proportional match or, in some cases, exceeded the challenge. If the pace of change has increased, so has the pace of *us*.

With that said, while writing this book the world has been hit by a global pandemic, a respiratory disease known as Covid-19, from a coronavirus. In many countries the attempts to manage it have required people to stay at home, putting economic and social life on hold. Very few have experience of such outbreaks to draw upon, and therefore the impact, short or longer term, is uncertain. Only when control is eventually secured will we see whether life will revert to the patterns with which we're familiar, or whether society will have changed irrevocably. Or a mix of both.

THE FORCE AND COMPLEXITY OF CHANGE RENDER US HELPLESS

That's to say, we can neither understand nor master the forces impacting our lives and are therefore mere pawns of predetermination. There are deep roots to this idea. The three Moirai – or Fate Spinners – of Ancient Greek mythology were believed to ensure that destiny as determined by eternal laws could operate without hindrance, even from the gods. Further, the Stoic movement, started by (the superbly named) Zeno in Athens in the 3rd century BCE, saw the universe as having one soul of which we're all a part and therefore unable to determine our own fate. Since these times we've never disproven our helplessness. Even if we decide to do something instinctively crazy at this very moment, it could be argued it was always intended to happen and that the notion of spontaneity is an illusion. It rather reduces the problem to absurdity.

Yet we can't – and don't – work like this. Imagine trying to argue it at an executive presentation. The Stoics also believed that how a person behaves illustrates far more about them than what they say (which we'll cover in Part Three). It presupposes we're freely able to make choices that will determine an outcome, for ourselves and others. We're forever identifying desirable destinations and planning how we're going to get there, from everyday minutiae to the seismic in our lives. We firmly believe in doing so that we have control, whatever may arise. Robert Louis Stevenson once said "to travel hopefully is a better thing than to arrive"[3] – yet we enjoy both. We'll always be travelling somewhere, but getting there can be rewarding, too. At least before we inevitably start off for somewhere else.

WE CHANGE IN A PREDICTABLE CURVE

It would be almost impossible to write a book about change without mentioning the 'Grieving Curve,' created by the Swiss-American psychiatrist Elisabeth Kübler-Ross in her 1969 book *On Death and Dying*.[4] On a personal level, leaving this mortal coil is as fundamental a change as we can encounter. The now-famous curve, illustrating the five stages of emotion through which Kübler-Ross observed terminally ill patients passing, has over time somehow slipped from its original purpose to being commonly recognized as the 'change curve' – quite a shift. There are seemingly a multitude of variants, so in Figure 1 I've created one based on the Wikipedia version[5] (the short explanations are mine, as they might apply to a change initiative).

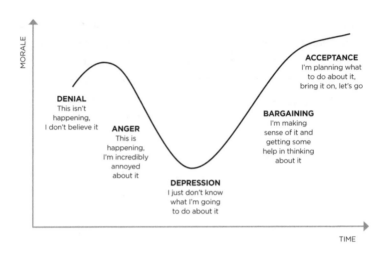

FIGURE 1

Before considering its value to our understanding of change, it's worth bearing in mind that Kübler-Ross later noted that the stages weren't necessarily a linear progression, even though they're shown as such and have hence been interpreted this way. That's the first reason for setting it aside for our purposes here. It may be enough on its own, but there are others. We'll briefly mention three.

First, while proportionally some or all of these emotions may be experienced during a change initiative, if it were that straightforward, then planning would be a breeze. I could sign off here. We'd know exactly what to do and when, with a predictable outcome at each stage. Second, we certainly don't always throw our colleagues into a state of instant denial the moment the change initiative is made known. Sometimes the change we are proposing is welcomed, and the emotion unleashed is joyful exuberance. Finally, the curve is hugely disempowering. It depicts us as helpless (as with the last myth), in dire need of change being done for (and to) us. We have no part to play, input to provide or opportunity to shape the outcome. Which renders the whole process rather depressing from start to finish.

For these reasons, we can leave the model to the field in which it began: it's not for us.

WHY CHANGE?

"If we possess our why of life we can put up with almost any how."
Friedrich Nietzsche[6]

THE RATIONALE

There was a particular chap in my organization who wasn't up for changing. The expressionless looks suggested he had dispensed with any emotional connection that may have offered us a glimmer of hope. His eyes were dark, his lips pressed. His heels were dug in as far as the igneous layer. The present way of working was so ideally cast that there could be no possible advantage in a new approach. He didn't want to hear reason, as to him it was unreasonable.

When the realization happened for him, he was the tree falling in the forest that no one heard. It was several months after the formal migration. He reached the decision to change on his own. Shortly afterward he approached me in the staff café and said, without a hint of formality, "You know, I was wrong. I'm sorry I was so damn difficult. All the time. But I could never go back to the way I used to work. Thank you." We shared a moment of rewind and erase (it's a generational thing) and a long smile. We didn't speak of it again.

This was many years ago and a formative interaction. It was neither a change management success nor failure. We didn't somehow 'win' at last, neither did he relent or submit to inevitability. This was when I understood that everyone changes at their own pace. People change themselves. Our role is to provide the resources, knowledge and opportunity to allow people to do so. They may not change on our imposed timescale, they may not "get with the programme," as every programme is artificial. There are, in fact, as many programmes as there are people, plus one. They're all as important as each other.

Overall, we don't have a change 'problem.' The likelihood of success or failure may well be subject to "the cumulative effects of randomness"[7] – that is, the normal distribution. We can't know or prove that, of course. The chance of mastering change is, as we shall explore, limited by the nature of change itself. Sometimes we'll smash it, sometimes we'll think we may have disturbed a ley line and it smashes us. Most of the time we'll achieve a degree of satisfaction. Yet we can always do better. That means equipping ourselves to do better.

As such there isn't exactly a gap in a crowded market for a book about change. At least not an immediately noticeable one. There are plenty of rich and informed texts to choose from, and I've massive respect for anyone who has tried to write about this incredibly amorphous subject. An evaluation of them all is beyond the scope of this book. Yet somehow none of those I've read capture the essence of the exchange with which this chapter began.

I'm not offering an approach to change that I believe is superior to any other, but an alternative that's logical, accessible and easy to practice. My first stab at doing so was as a more concise guide. Yet the limitations squeezed out the space needed for the unpredictable, wilful and contradictory nature of *us*. When W.C. Fields famously advised us to never work with animals or children, he might have included adults. So I removed the constraints and let it work itself out as it was needed.

Sometimes when considering change advice, we could be forgiven for thinking that the environment in which we operate is one of controlled laboratory conditions. Actors behave rationally and considerately, things happen as expected, moved around on a tabletop chart with croupier sticks. Generally, therefore, it's how we think and plan. If we just think and plan *enough*, we can iron out the randomness. We may consider motives and agendas, but when we move more than one diminished probability or dependent assumption away it all gets rather uncomfortable. We also feel that if we base our plans on logic and reason, we can't be held responsible when the unexpected happens. Which, of course, it invariably does, and we are.

The Ancient Greeks were incredibly smart. It could have been 'first-mover advantage' or the now-legendary Mediterranean (or even Aegean) diet. Perhaps it was a product of their rather shambolic societal institutions forcing them to argue incessantly, such that they became rather good at it. For the Sophists it even became a profession, being paid to take a contrary view with anyone about anything. From this age of carved fragments and retold stories, in thinking about change, Heraclitus stands out. Writing in Ephesus around the mid-6th century BCE he famously (among a small but committed crowd) asserted that – as the simplified version runs, to suit modern understanding – "we never step twice in the same river."[8] That is, as we contemplate even the most sluggish brook from one moment to the next, both the water and we have moved on. We're both different. It's a simple and pervasive idea. Nothing ever stands still, everything flows. Or 'panta rhei' as he would have said it in Greek. Accepting this makes planning or doing anything decidedly awkward.

THE ACTORS

So, we're outside the laboratory and on the streets.

At this stage it's worth establishing some terms as they relate to the actors within a change initiative. These may not be universal, as labels are always applied in context, but they're those I see most regularly. There are three broadly defined key roles:

- The **Change Leader**, at a senior level within the organization (usually director or executive) with a specific existing strategic role, and the person primarily responsible for its success.

- The **Change Manager**, at a relatively senior level with a specific existing tactical or operational role, and the person primarily responsible for making it happen. It can sometimes be an interim role, for the duration of the initiative (and quite often in this regard starting too late and ending too early, as Part One will help explain). In particularly large or technical initiatives, the role may be wholly focused on change, with the tactical and operational responsibilities passed to others.

- The **Change Consultant** (or Advisor), usually an external party (occasionally internal) whose main discipline is organizational change, and whose role is to advise the Change Manager and Change Leader on how to make the initiative a success. They may have relevant subject matter expertise or specialize in a specific area or type of change. They usually have a favoured change methodology – or one that the market requires they hold a qualification in.

We can typically (but not exclusively) characterize their differences, as in Table 1.

	CHANGE LEADER	CHANGE MANAGER	CHANGE CONSULTANT
Position/level	Executive or senior management	Senior or middle management	External, with relevant experience
Contribution	Responsibility	Delivery	Advice
Time allocated	Moderate	Extensive	Limited
Type of activity	Strategic	Tactical/ operational	Advisory
Primary expertise	Specific profession, industry/sector and leadership	Specific profession, industry/sector and management	Change – possibly discipline, industry or sector
Change expertise	Initiative-specific, mid- and senior level	Initiative-specific, mid-level	Extensive and varied
Interactions	Colleagues affected Senior leadership	Colleagues affected Change champions	Project team Change Manager
Responsibility	Full Overall success	Planning Execution	High quality and timely advice

TABLE 1

Organizationally, it usually looks something like Figure 2 (the arrows represent reporting lines).

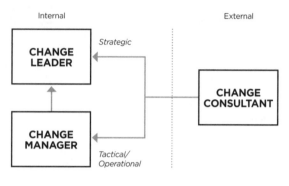

FIGURE 2

Some clarifications are necessary, to emphasize how confusing this can all become. 'Change Leader' and 'Change Manager' are usually designations in regard to the initiative rather than formally ascribed job titles. Those concerned already have such. Sometimes, where the scale dictates, the Change Manager and Change Leader roles are one. 'Change Consultant' is usually a self-ascribed term – sometimes 'Change Manager' is used instead. The Change Consultant can on occasions be asked to deliver the change, acting as the Change Manager. However, this may be regarded negatively as it creates the impression that change is being 'done to' those within the organization by an external party. This, in turn, tees up the Consultant as the scapegoat if something goes awry. So, that's all crystal clear, then.

We're likely to encounter two other prominent support- ing roles. First, **change sponsors** – these are mentioned more fully in the section 'Making stuff happen: managing and leading' in the 'Local thinking' chapter in Part One. They're not included here as they're not considered to be main characters – sponsorship is more of a supporting role, albeit often vital. Second, **change recipients**, those respon- sible for enacting the change (or aspects of it) but not specifically for the design or leadership of the initiative. These include operational managers within departments directly involved and functions such as Legal, Finance and Human Resources.

There are roles associated with participation too, that we shall cover in Part Three – principally **change champions** and those associated with the governance of the initiative.

This book is for all three key roles, for different reasons. Change Consultants should be familiar with much of the material, albeit it may not represent their specific philosophy or approach. It may therefore provide some alternative perspectives or angles. For Change Managers, their specific experience of leading a change initiative may be limited and so both a high level and a detailed view may be helpful. For Change Leaders, the overall picture may be beneficial, and the practical contribution may assist with getting the best out of their team.

I shall use the term 'lead change' as the generic expression throughout the book, as it applies to the most overarching of the roles, that with the most responsibility attached.

THE NARRATOR

I'm a change practitioner several decades in. I've held all three of the key roles, yet I've always led, managed and advised on change in context, as a workstream within a profession. I imagine that the same applies to most of us. We're probably here because we've been asked to lead a change initiative, but change isn't how we'd instinctively describe *what we do*. I've spent a considerable portion of this time encouraging my colleagues to see themselves first as leaders of change and thereafter as specialists in their chosen field. That is, to consider their specialism as a downstream 'plug-in' to a change initiative, and not the all-too-common reverse.

It's a fundamental shift. Understanding that change is our primary role, rather than secondary, is vital in helping us understand and navigate just about every challenge that comes our way.

As a practitioner I'm not rigorous enough to be an academic (as my academic friends politely remind me) and not deep enough to be a philosopher (I'm sure if I knew any, they would remind me, too), yet I draw on both approaches. I offer a perspective on the realities of change sometimes not afforded to the observer on the hillside. There's a flavour of my approach in my first book *The Elemental Workplace*.[9] When talking about the physical environment we're dealing with tangibles – the *what*. While we explored the why and how, the ultimate end product was something we could experience with all our senses. We could read the book and know *what* we had to create. With change it's not quite so straightforward.

Many views of successful organizational change are based on a list of things we must do, in some form of sequential order, instructed at each instance from above. As Khurshed Dehnugara and Claire Genkai Breeze lament, "we have come to accept that a logical ordered approach from the top down is the gold standard of creating change."[10] It often looks something like Figure 3.

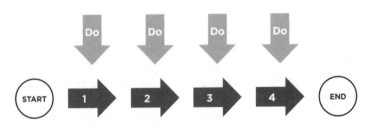

FIGURE 3

It's naive, unrealistic and brittle. It plays to a bygone era of sheltered subservience and cascaded responsibility, where the fault only ever lies in execution. That is, in the lower reaches of the pyramid. The reality of our world – as will be explored in Part One of this book – is far more organic. While we need to do things, we need to have both an underlying philosophy that enables us to think, act and respond, as well as an adaptable preparatory structure that equips us to face any type or scale of change challenge.

THE PLOT

I've used an approach popularized by Simon Sinek[11] but, as I recently discovered, that originated with Nietzsche as the opening quotation illustrates. Perhaps even earlier. Start with why, then how and finally what.

The approach to change I offer is simple: **reflect** (why are we doing this?), **prepare** (how are we going to do it?) and **act** (specifically, what are we going to do?). It's a model of readiness for all change initiatives to come, at any degree of imperative (when), scope (where) or scale (how much).

The reflection (the **why**) concerns our philosophical infrastructure, the foundation on which our approach is based. We must start with it to understand what we're doing and how we're doing it, or our actions (even if occasionally successful) are groundless. It comprises **three levels** of idea – universal, global and local. I've tried to keep it succinct and relatable. If the practical aspects of preparing for and delivering change are more enticing – we just want to *do* stuff – then skip it for now. Returning to it at the end is entirely workable. Graphically, it looks something like Figure 4:

FIGURE 4

The preparation (the **how**; Figure 5) is the operating system of change – the materials, resources and processes we need to be ready to lead change of any description or category. Little in the modern age works without an operating system. It's the code that sits between the operator and the hardware that makes the applications we use possible. Ours here is open source. There are **six components**. In Part Two we'll arrange them in a spider chart to illustrate their relationship.

FIGURE 5

The actions (the **what**; Figure 6) are the **nine elements** of change, born of three dimensions – information, engagement and involvement. They form a coherent whole. To a degree, dependent upon circumstances, we need to do each. They're both contents page and checklist. We'll arrange them in a periodic table in Part Three, to which the title of the book alludes, with meaning behind the rows ('periods') and columns ('groups').

FIGURE 6

Putting all three together, the overall change framework looks like Figure 7. They're arranged in what appears to be reverse order as 'Why?' is our infrastructure, our base layer, and we build from there:

WHAT are we going to do?	ACTION Elements of change	
HOW are we going to do it?	**PREPARATION** Operating system of change	
WHY are we doing this?	**REFLECTION** Infrastructure of change	

FIGURE 7

With this approach to change there's no critical path, there are no stones across the river. It doesn't provide all the answers, because I haven't got them. Your pattern of interest in this book will be unique to you, dependent on where you've come from, where you are and where you're heading. There will be ideas you'll wish I'd expanded on, those you'll wonder what are doing here, and some you'll disagree with entirely. My intention is to try to equip, not to solve. When you then bring your own insight, experience, instinct, relationships, character and motivation to bear it's likely you'll be incredibly successful. Think of this book not as a piece of the jigsaw but as the picture on the box, the guide to how it all fits together.

While I've woven stories through the book, taking care to try to avoid anyone recognizing themselves, it's without interviews and named case studies to avoid the perils of date-stamping and the fluctuating fortune of brands, operational and personal. While approaches and models come and go, unlike the physical environment in which it operates, change as a discipline is relatively free of the ravages of fad and fashion.

The book doesn't take itself *too* seriously. Seriously enough, given that for us, much is at stake. Obtaining help, though, needn't mean several qualifying rounds of intellectual gymnastics topped off with a take-home portion of imposter syndrome. I've tried to keep it grounded, accessible and encouraging. It should be both useful and enjoyable. I figure that if it's even some of the latter, it's likely to be a lot more of the former.

The elemental approach is intended to be relevant to the past (helping to understand what happened and why), present (usable now) and future (independent of the ideas and tools of the age) and applicable to any industry sector, physical location, culture, discipline or scale of initiative or investment.

My hope is that you find what follows as I've intended it to be – structured, relatable, straightforward, usable, universal and timeless. Moreover, it's a workbook. It's not intended to remain pristine. Make notes. Mess it up.

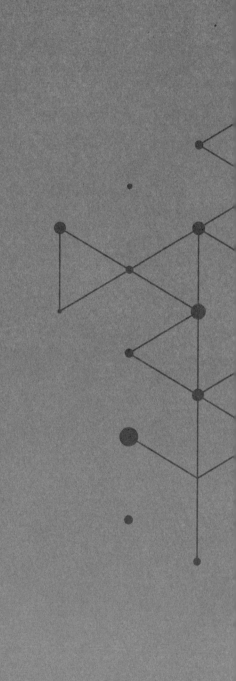

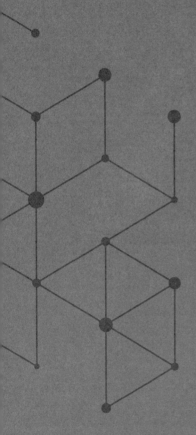

REFLECTION
WHY ARE WE DOING THIS?

THE INFRASTRUCTURE
OF CHANGE

We could just crash headlong into our change initiative, get cracking and make stuff happen even if the world doesn't stand still. When we look around, everyone else seems to be doing it.

A lot of people are talking about doing it, too: posts on social media decked in stock photography featuring stress-wrinkle-free foreheads, easy smiles and sparkling teeth, sanitized change effortlessly delivered to order. It can make us feel inadequate if we dwell on it. That's because the first point to consider with change is how it makes us feel as we contemplate what lies ahead.

CHANGE SCENARIOS

Through my career I've met and worked with people for whom change feels like one of these alternative scenarios. We'll see ourselves in these situations somewhere (although we probably won't want to say so):

- **An emergency.** We're on a burning platform, mostly fictitious – change, or die (horribly) – so do whatever it takes and do it now. It ends up being frenzied and chaotic, but the objective is achieved despite the ridiculous proportion of effort to productive outcome. When it's all done and celebrated, no one especially worries about that, believing that next time it'll be different – better planned, more economical, less stressful. The underlying philosophy, printed onto team T-shirts in Wham! sized letters is: "*JFDI!*"
- **Resistance mitigation.** It's a bulldozing. We'll get to the other end no matter who gets in the way. It's going to happen, and opposition is futile. Success is identified as a simple result – victory. Us versus them. There's emotion, and there are casualties (tears, resignations) on both sides. Existing relationships are broken, never to be repaired

and few new ones are created. The underlying philosophy mumbled at meetings is: *"You have to crack a few eggs if you want to make an omelette."* At the time of mumbling, no one knows who the eggs are. Everyone secretly wonders if it's them. And hopes not.

- **Repairs and maintenance.** A mechanical operation on a stationary object, safely isolated from the mains. We follow the manual, do what's required, reconnect and test. The process is highly linear, punctured by phase gates and signoffs, so completion is usually late and buried under a mountain of auditable paperwork. No one fiddles with the rest of the inactive object while we're performing our work. No one gets hurt and no one falls out, yet someone usually gets blamed for it being late. The underlying philosophy that starts each meeting is: *"Perfect planning prevents piss-poor performance."* It doesn't, of course.

- **A popularity contest.** We must do this, but please don't hate us! We do whatever it takes to keep others on our side. Resources include short-shelf-life charm and a jumbo order pad. Satisfaction becomes habituated and so it's over budget and late due to the scope-creep/stampede. Efforts to keep people happy usually result in not many people being especially happy. Recriminations include promises to be tougher next time. The underlying philosophy, printed onto team mugs is: *"Keep calm and carry on."* People really still do this.

- **A conspiracy.** We have to do this but there's another hidden agenda. It's just masking a more sinister aim, so we'll play along while we try to uncover what's really going on and find out who stands to gain. When we discover what it is, no one will believe us as the 'deep state' (corporate leadership) has its tentacles everywhere. We'll never know which side anyone is on. Leading change is a manicured pretence. We grin and bear it, all the while looking over our shoulder, trying to work out who's lurking in the shadows.

The underlying philosophy, barely whispered to anyone, is: *"Trust no one."* So, no one does.

- **A tragicomedy.** It's going to be awful, but if we can laugh at ourselves, we may just survive. The laughing usually begins too soon. The entrenched cynicism wafting around culture and process means it never stands a chance. It happens on time and on budget, but the tragedy outweighs the comedy, and when it's all done everyone just feels as though they let themselves down. The underlying philosophy, printed onto team coasters, is: *"You don't have to be mad to work here, but it helps."* It actually doesn't help.

- **A steeplechase.** A defined linear route, with a few hurdles and a water jump, that we can train for and will get to the end of puffed out, with wet feet and a twisted ankle, but happy. It has the whiff of spirited amateurism about it, all rather gallant, effort over craft. Some of the workarounds will look odd and fail, but no one will mind as long as someone had a go. The underlying philosophy, concluding a reassuring leadership briefing when the team look a bit frazzled, is: *"Worse things happen at sea."* Yes, they do. But they needn't happen here.

Of course, we're likely to experience change as one or more of these scenarios at varying times on the path. None of the above are necessarily wrong, but they're all rather negative. In each, there's an assumption that change is a burden, something to get through or be overcome. We're apprehensive, queasy, empty. The whirlpool of emotion doesn't make us want to do it, and sure as heck doesn't make us want to lead it.

It needn't be this way.

OUR INFRASTRUCTURE

We can, instead, consider change as an opportunity, unfolding through a clear vision of what can be achieved. It'll entail a mix of certainty and uncertainty, in which we'll have an openness to the unexpected. We'll know what to do and how to do it. We'll be equipped and ready, positive and confident. We'll actually *look forward to it*.

To take this approach, before leaping into the disorienting complexity of organizational dynamics, we first need a robust understanding of what we're dealing with. That is, the stuff that helps us see change in the manner described rather than in terms of any of the scenarios with which the chapter began. It will help us explore and understand the reason why we're doing it at all, and why we'll need to do it in a particular way to stand the greatest chance of being successful. We may call this the infrastructure of change, the foundation of everything that happens. Not in the form of steel, concrete and wires, but a rich body of ever-developing thinking that gives us the confidence to plan and act.

There are three interrelated levels:

- **The universal**: fundamental ideas that apply to everything and everyone, here and beyond, regardless. They're incontrovertible, we can't argue them away. They're arrayed over us like the starry firmament. In philosophical terms, 'metaphysical.'
- **The global**: ideas relating to the way things are on this planet, with a grounding in practical reality. They're everywhere we look and turn.
- **The local**: ideas relating to organizations and people at a commonly understood, human level. They relate to us, those around us and the organizations to which we belong, irrespective of type, sector or location.

We're subject to them all, and they're always moving. Sometimes they're aligned, mostly they're not. It's why in Figure 4 they're each shown in an orbit around us. We'll consider them in turn.

UNIVERSAL THINKING

The ideas we're classing as universal might be termed first principles. As with many such notions, we usually take the reality we perceive for granted and move to the next, more tangible level. If the universal stuff just *is*, then there's nothing we can do about it. But knowing and thinking about it is important. It's worth the investment.

ALL IS FLUX

Change is our very essence. As physical beings we're constantly consuming, replicating and shedding until we're no more. Nothing about us is ever static. Not only *are* we constantly changing but we *want* things to change. We're inherently unsatisfied. We set goals, ambitions, targets. We're always casting hooks into the future, hauling ourselves forward. For us, change is both reality and aspiration in equal measure.

While at times there may be things with which we're happy and we would like to stay the same, this doesn't equate to a fear or dislike of 'change.' As pattern-seeking creatures we recognize that routine is helpful, so we do all we can to make our lives easier. We're predisposed to finding workarounds. It frees time to focus on the stuff we find more interesting. By doing so we lift the anxiety and no longer feel overwhelmed. At least, until the next email. In its turn each instance of this is a mere fragment of our lives and ourselves.

Heraclitus maintained that the very nature of life is change or 'flux,' as he put it. If we resist this truth (which would be futile), it's to resist ourselves, and he reassured us that we do so only because we don't understand that life is change. That is, it only hurts because we don't get it. We're therefore never in a state of *being*, but rather always in a state of *becoming*. It means there's no such thing as the 'status quo.' The phrase *ceteris paribus* (all other things being equal), often used by lawyers and scientists, is nothing more than a theoretical construct and 'steady state' just means a period of very little, or very low, change (in scale or frequency).

While change may be intangible, we can deploy techniques to help us make sense of it.

We can describe a change as the *difference* between one state and another. 'State' in this case is temporary, a snapshot.

We can measure the *distance* between the two (temporary) states and quantify or qualify it.

We can do all we can to make the *process* of moving from one state to another quicker, easier, more interesting, and less fraught with risk or danger.

However, in every instance we're capturing what change means to us in terms of something else. While it's both tricky and at the same time liberating, it's an essential tenet.

In thinking about our change initiative, change isn't something to fear – it's our essence. We're predisposed toward it. We mustn't defeat ourselves before we've begun.

PERPETUAL BETA

If everything flows, then nothing is ever started or finished. There's no enduring and predictable normality to which we return for safety. The end of one thing is inherently the start of something else, and vice versa. We're living an experiment.

We have a modern way to look at it. In the world of product development and, in particular, software, there are three forms of trialling before the device or program is released to the market: alpha, beta and gamma. We don't talk much about alpha testing because it's performed behind closed doors. It's where a product is around three quarters done and is tested by the technical experts looking for glitches or bugs. It hasn't left the lab yet. Beta trialling is where it's tested by those who'll use or consume it. It's around four fifths complete and there may only be a few corners that need chamfering – there shouldn't be anything serious or existential left to resolve. We don't talk about gamma testing much either, the final safety check, which in an incurably impatient world has almost disappeared or been rolled into alpha and beta.

The idea of 'perpetual beta' comes from IT guru Tim O'Reilly, who also gave us the term 'open source' software.[12] It's been harnessed by others, noticeably in the work of learning consultant Harold Jarche.[13] It started life as the expression and practice "release early, release often." The notion has morphed into "fail fast, fail often" as a mantra for trying things. It's mostly applied to software because where it's a subscription-based service ('Software as a Service' – or SaaS) rather than a product delivered in a cellophane-wrapped box and loaded via a CD-ROM, improvements and upgrades are automatically sent to all subscribers. The consumer effectively invests in both the service as-is at the time of commitment, and the developments to come, the service of the future.

We've become entirely familiar, formally and informally, with incremental software release numbering. We commonly use three digits to denote the changes – Major.Minor.Patch. Sometimes we manage to leap stages. There is no planned end number. The only destination we're trying to reach is better.

With this mindset we're not afraid to see if something may work, as we think there's a good chance it will. As the consumer is using a product or service at a stage of development, they become part of the design process and are treated as a co-developer. An effective feedback loop is therefore vital. There's no point experimenting if we don't know whether it's worked – and if it hasn't, why not.

It's easy to get cynical about a methodology that has the potential to rationalize slapdash inefficiency and reward non-achievement. However, it's not all just consequence-free irresponsibility; sooner or later something meaningful must emerge on which to build, or it's bust. Failing too fast and too often isn't viable. In many ways this mirrors the evolution of the natural world, the clearest example of *panta rhei*.

We usually draw the line at experimentation with mission-critical activities, but all this means is that the testing becomes far more stringently alpha than beta. Wherever our change project lies on a scale of mission criticality, the same principles apply. It just becomes a question of how far upstream we experiment, and to what degree the consumer will be invited to take part.

Our change initiative relates to something – a system, process, structure or physical entity – that appears static but is, in fact, in a state of perpetual beta. Our initiative accelerates this natural flow. It gives it purpose and direction and defines it.

What this also means is that through our open channel of dialogue and iterative development we are operating in a mode of continual evaluation. We touch on post-initiative review in the Close but the on-going nature of this approach means there will be considerably less pressure on the need for large-scale and formal 'pre' and 'post' assessments and the surprises that often lurk within.

We use another convenience here, too – adding markers in time, or bookends. In the same way that for ease we imagine change to be a thing, so we insert a defined start and finish line for comfort and certainty. That they mean something to us and those affected is enough. Yet they don't dam the flow, which moves right on through the bookends regardless.

In thinking about our change initiative, we're creating a version of our intended outcome, something that will only ever be a work-in-progress, that we'll allow to improve and develop over time. We should invite the consumers of our creation to actively contribute – and listen to them. We then all own it.

EVOLUTION AND TRANSFORMATION

In the way we speak in an organizational environment, our change initiative may seem to involve a strategic choice between being a larger-than-life, pumped up, charisma-oozing, bold transformation or a cautious, pragmatic, less-nourished and careful evolution. It's the gladiator versus the accountant, tridents versus spreadsheets. Yet the initiative is invariably *dressed up* in the gladiator's garb of transformation even when underneath it's an accountant, because it more widely resonates. It's likely to win followers, even devotees.

There's no need to choose. They're intrinsically related.

In the biological sense, transformation occurs when a cell consumes another cell and the two become one. The voracious cell doesn't know whether it'll be a good thing before it happens. It doesn't perform a risk assessment and weigh up the pros and cons. It's a single cell, so it just does it. Hang the consequences. Most such transformations are terminal. It's a one-off, highly dangerous single step – immediately after which, the highest risk period occurs. Yet it holds the seed of infinite possibilities, a true *what if?* moment. In the natural world, transformation along with reproduction and a huge slice of luck equals evolution.

Businesses often transform themselves by consuming something like another business. It's usually (but not always) a little more informed a decision, but it's still dangerous and sometimes terminal. The DNA (comprising people, mission, culture, values, processes and technology) doesn't always mix, even if it suggested it would 'on paper.'

Transformation isn't bigger than evolution even if it's a bigger-sounding word that we've progressively inflated over time. It's the opposite. With the two ideas, it's their *nature* not their *size* that defines them. Evolution is the long game, punctuated by many transformations. Transformations are the risk-imbued shifts that make step-changes in progress possible.

If transformation is a leap in the dark, evolution inherently builds on what's working. It's why change approaches such as Solutions Focus and Appreciative Inquiry (AI, just to confuse) often appeal. Both reject the problem-orientation often instilled within us from our earliest education and, instead, look to discover and define what's working with the intent of doing more of it. Even when a system or process appears to be failing dramatically, there's usually *something* that's working that offers a starting point for resolving it.

That doesn't stop anyone using the term transformation to describe a bold series of events rolling up to an overall vision. Nor is it necessarily wrong. If it creates courage when it's needed, it's serving its purpose. The point is more to elevate the idea of evolution, to slip it out of its crumpled pinstriped suit. The biological basis for the term unfortunately tends to lead us to considering the million years it takes a snake to grow legs. Evolution in our case can be accelerated. It helps frame transformative steps in terms of need and relevance.

In thinking about our change initiative, given that everything flows and therefore exists in a state of perpetual beta, our change initiative is by nature an evolution – potentially, of course, with some transformational steps. We may, however, still want to call it a transformation.

ADAPTATION AND ADOPTION

Unlike evolution and transformation, we often use adaptation and adoption interchangeably, but they're different. Sometimes an expression is well-worn and so we just use it as we hear it – like 'early adopter.' How often do we hear 'early adapter'? I'm indebted to my friend Luis Suarez,[14] social business and technology guru, for the benefit of his wisdom in a long discussion on the difference between these two terms.

With **adoption** we take on something additional, as it is. It may mean losing something else to accommodate it, but it's a bolt-on, nonetheless. Like downloading an application to a smartphone. There's little need to break stride, it's just with us. The trouble is it can be just as easily offloaded if we can't find a use for it. We may not give it a fair crack and just decide we don't want it. Its worth usually has to be established quickly.

Adoption is useful when an existential urgency exists (do it or perish), where speed is essential or where the change is simple (even huge simple). There's a satisfying sense of immediacy that meets with our impatience. It feels like it fits a programme. We can set a required-by date. If this appears at risk, it's simply a case of adding proportionally more effort. Or changing the date.

Yet where there's any degree of complexity at all, adoption invariably achieves only a short-term success. New behaviours, systems or processes requested are tried before a reversion to the previous ways of doing things. Consequently, it's often a defensive approach to change.

Adoption needs rules, too, as the change required is man-ufactured. The resulting output of many initiatives is a new set of protocols and policies designed to govern behaviour, to create the adhesion needed. They very often work to a logic that runs: if we can get people to do x [new behaviour] then y [benefit] results. We too often try to change the way people are rather than designing for the way they might become.

With **adaptation** we alter something, such as the circum-stances needed to accommodate it. It's a step in evolution, like an upgrade to our smartphone's operating system. Once we've adapted, it's highly probable that the changes made will remain and evolve further. If we move to a way of doing things that appears similar to a past method, we don't adapt *back*, we adapt *again*. It just so happens our new state may bear a similarity to a previous state. Evolution doesn't work in reverse.

Adaptation-oriented change programmes instinctively feel slower and less defined as an allowance for personal time is required. We're asking the human to reprogram themselves while they're busy being a human. It isn't instantaneous. We can play to its strengths, however, and gear a change initiative toward adaptation in the first place, rather than hurling a multitude of things to be adopted and hoping some stick.

Adaptation needs far fewer – if any – rules. Compulsion isn't required when the change has been rationalized and fully absorbed. We don't need to tell people to do something when they already do it, want to do it and don't want to do what they did before. And who needs more rules in their life?

Adoption and adaptation *can* work together if we understand the difference.

There's a window of opportunity in which adoption can be converted to adaptation. Having adopted something new, if it's explored thoroughly, we may adapt *to* the use of the new idea, technology or tool and alter the way we do or see things as a result. The preposition 'to' is the critical difference. We adopt *x*, we adapt *to y*. When we adapt it necessitates movement, our position changes. Yet this isn't achieved by applying the pressure associated with protocols and deadlines. Adoption is far more likely to work when embedded within an adaptive approach.

We may, for instance, after a sustained campaign by a friend adopt a vegan lifestyle for its potential environmental and health benefits. One fine day we simply give up eating meat and wearing leather shoes. There's a period of vulnerability as we try and adjust the habits and preferences accumulated over a lifetime. Our friend moves from light humour to annoying exasperation as we grapple clumsily with the new way of life. We may create for ourselves the time and patience to learn and embrace it, to adapt to it. Or, tired of being judged and nagged, we may just head for the Argentine steakhouse and think about what might have been.

There are a number of approaches to management and leadership in use prefixed with 'adaptive' that have proven successful, and that touch on several themes in this book. It's not possible to review them here. They're best explored and enjoyed over a double espresso or two.

In thinking about our change initiative, change is movement, not simply adhesion. We need to identify and create adaptation strategies, providing the time and resources to allow people to change themselves.

BUTTERFLIES, BUTTERFLIES

We've all likely heard of the 'butterfly effect,' a metaphor developed by meteorologist Edward Lorenz and published in 1963,[15] building on the earlier ideas of French mathematician and engineer Henri Poincaré[16] and some literary roots deeper in time. It supposes that a butterfly flapping its wings on one side of the world might cause a tornado on the other. That is, small things can have a big effect when everything is connected. It's all part of chaos theory. That chaos has a theory at all seems inherently wrong.

We often spend far too much time trying to predict the future, but too little shaping or creating it. What we've covered so far is enough to extract the notion that there are some underlying patterns in our lives, just not enough for confidently predicting the future. This is both good and bad news for leading change. It means there's some hope for creating a clear path to a successful outcome, but a high likelihood of unforeseen circumstances along the way. We'd have to count ourselves unlucky if one of them was a tornado.

Our universe, the whole interconnected ecosystem, is a mesh of almost infinite 'complex adaptive systems' (CAS). Interestingly, and supportive of what was discussed earlier in Part One, they aren't called 'adoptive' systems. A 'system' in this sense can be a city, an organization, an animal colony – anything that appears coherent as an entity that's made up of a number of parts or components dynamically interacting with one another. What the parts of the system do doesn't tell us what the whole thing will do. Tiny events like those of the butterfly cause the overall system to self-organize and change. Rather than causing a tornado, our red admiral is more likely to flap a tiny contribution, yet one that irrevocably evolves the system. Now consider a billion butterflies flapping their wings at the same time, and when they stop another billion flapping theirs. The systems never rest.

CYNEFIN AND CHAOS

The Cynefin framework (pronounced kuh-NEV-in), developed by Dave Snowden while at IBM in 1999,[17] tries to help. A Welsh word meaning 'habitat,' it's an intriguing sense-making tool that offers us a place to stand in viewing the situation confronting us. It has a fascinating story of how it came to be, too.[18] I've created a version of the Cynefin framework in Figure 8, in keeping with the graphical style of this book.

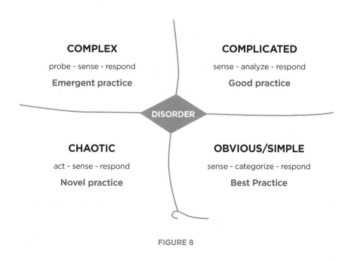

COMPLEX

probe - sense - respond

Emergent practice

COMPLICATED

sense - analyze - respond

Good practice

DISORDER

CHAOTIC

act - sense - respond

Novel practice

OBVIOUS/SIMPLE

sense - categorize - respond

Best Practice

FIGURE 8

Overlaid on the perennial threat of disorder are four domains or standpoints. The **obvious** is where rules are in existence and the relationship between cause and effect is simple. Where we move to the **complicated**, cause and effect require analysis or expertise to evaluate. By the time we're in the **complex** domain we're seeing cause and effect only in retrospect, while in the **chaotic**, cause and effect are entirely estranged. Disorder lurks beneath them all.

We're reminded here (for better or worse) of former US Secretary of Defense Donald Rumsfeld with his now-legendary 'known knowns' (obvious and complicated, in respect of the framework), 'known unknowns' (complex) and 'unknown unknowns' (chaotic), articulated in a speech in 2002.[19] Interestingly, the philosopher Slavoj Žižek has noted[20] that possibly more damaging are the 'unknown knowns,' the products of denial or amnesia. No doubt all of this finds its roots in the Johari Window created by psychologists Joseph Luft and Harrington Ingham in 1955.[21]

When we consider most scenarios we face, they comprise multiple layers and components in which we're sensing, analysing, categorizing, probing and acting. The interconnectedness of all things renders all situations inherently chaotic, with complex, complicated and simple elements that may – and often do – help us see and navigate them consciously and unconsciously. A single Cynefin domain may not be enough to help us make sense of the entirety. We may also wonder where we find room in such a model for the possible contribution of luck – pure random chance.

Therefore, we might playfully redraw it, using the four domains, as something more fluid. It's shown in Figure 9 (with apologies to Dave). In relation to a particular situation, we make sense of it through an interplay between all four domains, with the degree of each varying in size. It may be possible for one domain to be entirely dominant with mere traces of the others. Of course, they may be the same size, too.

The situation is unlikely to remain static and so we'll see the size of each increasing and decreasing at varying stages. The outer edge of the scenario is a broken line, to show that it will not be entirely self-contained. Lurking beneath – rather than disorder – is chance.

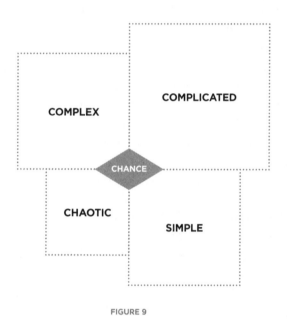

FIGURE 9

It's worth us considering some recent challenges we've faced against this model, to establish whether what occurred was what was expected. We're no strangers to proclaiming, "I knew that would happen!" when something goes wrong. Of course, we didn't. It's just that our retrospective pessimism softens the blow by aligning it with inevitability.

UNCERTAINTY

Change by its nature creates uncertainty. That is, a sense that things can't be relied on to happen or to be what they might be expected to be. It's an inherent characteristic of complex systems.

Unlike chaos, however, with which it's often associated, uncertainty presents discoverable patterns, scenarios and relationships we can recognize and use to create stability. The redrawn model in Figure 9 allows us to reduce the chaos in any given situation, potentially squeezing it to a minimum. The resulting environment is instead one of varying degrees of uncertainty.

Uncertainty also isn't the same as risk, covered in Part Two. Risk is a situation involving exposure to a *known* danger. We assess the chances of the danger (something happening, or not happening) being realized and do what we can to mitigate or remove the risk. We try not to negatively impact the desirable aspects of the situation. To manage it, we *plan* for it. With uncertainty, however, we often don't know what will occur. This means we need to *prepare* for it rather than plan. We may therefore think of uncertainty as the parent, and risk as the troublesome offspring.

We usually see certainty as a desirable thing. We believe it better helps us identify and remove risk. We associate it with being able to get things done, so we try all we can to create it. If everything is predictable, we can confidently model the future.

The trouble is that if all things happen as they should and are expected to, nothing *interesting* happens. Despite the aura of negativity that surrounds uncertainty, the outcome might just as likely be good as bad. The philosopher Nietzsche welcomed uncertainty. It may even be said he craved it, proclaiming that "No doubt, certainty is what drives one insane."[22] He believed that the measure of the worth of a person was the amount of uncertainty they were able to bear. Incidentally, his life ended with him insane, but it's doubtful it was the certainty that got him there.

Fortunately, absolute certainty is a theoretical possibility only. We need balance; *some* certainty, in the right areas, but only just enough. Uncertainty creates the opportunity for change.

HEURISTICS

In dealing with uncertainty, a key technique for making decisions that has evolved with us is heuristics. A heuristic is a shortcut deployed where there's a lot of information to process or little time, to do so, or both, often referred to as 'rule of thumb.' The approach was especially useful for our hunter-gatherer ancestors in quickly assessing opportunities (to eat) and risk (of being eaten). While there are advantages of making and testing decisions at speed, embedding such an approach within a sympathetic and supportive framework such as Agile (that we shall cover in Part Two), if it were that easy to solve problems we could dispense with more rigorous and time-consuming approaches. In our haste we can as easily succumb to bias or errors in judgment as we can break through a fug of ponderance. That said, there's just as much a place for heuristics in the modern world as there was in antiquity, as long as it's not the only approach. Uncertainty doesn't have it all its own way.

In thinking about our change initiative, we could view all this as daunting in terms of our chances of success. We are, after all, flapping an enormous butterfly wing of our own making amid an ever evolving and connected world. Or we could see it as a pulsing energy, a natural movement that defies inertia. One that absorbs and converts the energy of resistance, that fashions untold possibilities from uncertainty, that feeds our desire to make things happen. All we need to do is tap into the source and find the channels. It's the lifeblood of optimism.

All the beguiling nuances and complexities of this chapter are with us, working to our advantage, if we want them to be. There's a poetry in change, and we're going to find it.

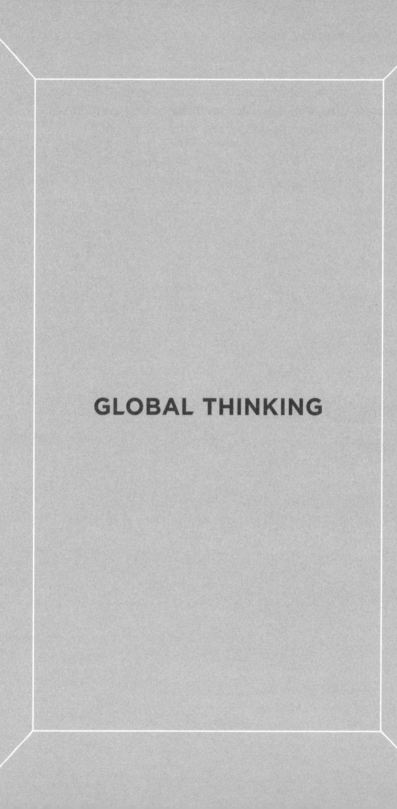

GLOBAL THINKING

The ideas I term 'global' are all around us, yet more rooted in practical reality than the universal. They are each a direct consequence of our universal thinking.

OUR *WELTANSCHAUUNG*

Our *Weltanschauung* is our comprehensive world view. While the translation is literal, in the German original it's an entire, all-encompassing framework through which we see and make sense of the world. It weaves together history, culture, language, philosophy, art, religion and education among other things. We then add our personal weighting drawn from learning, observation, perception and experience. The German term has a little more of 'life, the universe and everything' about it than the English 'world view,' but from here we'll revert to the latter.

Our world view remains buried in our subconscious, helping to direct and determine our values (what we permit our self to do) and actions (what we actually do) from its pivotal position. As the French philosopher Montesquieu said, "If triangles had a god, they would give him three sides."[23] It explains to us why things happen and why they happen the way they do. In times of particular stress or crisis we may surface and question some or all of it. At least we hope we'd do so.

Given that the influences upon it are broad, a world view is often shared by groups at a societal level. Its evolution is rarely fast enough to span a change initiative. Physical divides may seem trivial but can be highly significant. Something possible on one side of a border post or river may be impossible on the other. Yet there may not always be something as neat as a tangible boundary.

In leading change, we therefore have to understand the effect that our own world view has on the judgments we form, the views we take, and the inherent conscious and unconscious bias that it may reinforce, in addition to that of each of those impacted by our initiative individually and collectively. Seeing through not just the eyes but the entire frame of reference of others, avoiding interference from our own, is far from easy.

Starting with our world view helps us understand how it works. We might run some scenarios and consider what our reaction might be and why. It will then enable us to be more attuned to how it affects those who are subject to our initiative. It's unlikely we'll change their world view at any point, but we may at least begin to appreciate what's possible and what isn't.

In thinking about our change initiative, we're all looking through a lens we've (had) created, and so we'll all see the world differently. Understanding how will help guide us and others.

OUR LANDSCAPE

While we're looking at the world in a particular way, lots of stuff is happening within it.

We're about to explore a change initiative that we hope we can, by and large, control. Yet every initiative exists within a wider environment where we can only be aware of the complex forces at play, yet barely influence them. We're not going to try to mimic King Cnut ordering the tide to go back (albeit he was helpfully demonstrating to his court that he didn't have the power to do so). About all we can do with the wider landscape in which we're operating is a little light gardening.

This doesn't mean we're accepting that it's a VUCA world (volatile, uncertain, complex and ambiguous). There's now a myriad of management strategies based on VUCA, accepting and using its assumptions as a response toolkit. But VUCA is a pessimist's manifesto, straight out of military planning (it was first used in the US Army War College in the late 1990s[24]): if crazy stuff we don't and can't understand can happen any time, we need more tanks and bombs.

I do believe we're better than that. The world may not quite be stable, certain, understandable and lucid (SCUL, anyone?), but it's far from the Eliot-esque desert depicted in his 1922 poem *The Waste Land* that we've convinced ourselves envelopes us. We need to remember what resources we have to counteract VUCA, too: instantly accessible information on almost anything we need, the gift economy of advice and guidance (one of the most important contributions social media has made), less pressure from dogma and collective ignorance (politics aside) with a correspondingly healthier desire to discover for ourselves, a greater ability to travel and experience difference first hand (and still be home in time for tea) and ready access to the experience of others from which to learn. Our filters may be challenged like never before to ensure we're maintaining an open mind and not simply constructing an echo chamber for our world view, but just as the potential threat to stability may have grown so, proportionally, has our ability to counter it.

We're contending with the likes of: geopolitics; global trade and markets; access to capital; the supply, cost and availability of raw materials; the qualifications, location, motivation and availability of labour; climate change (or, more accurately, emergency); available and emerging technology and automation; and the fickle nature of brand in a world of instant and often emotional evaluation (usually simply termed 'ratings'). Some of these forces that are almost entirely out of our control may well impact our change initiative. They're not a list of excuses ready for post-rationalization, but a schedule of things to be aware of in advance and to monitor during.

The essential recourse is to know our environment. It sounds blindingly obvious but is often blindsiding. It means reading and listening beyond our normal probable boundaries. It's an investment. It doesn't mean checking our Twitter feed 300 times a day. Social media has its uses, but it isn't news. Even if none of the factors happens to affect our initiative, we'll have a much wider range of conversation than we started with – there's no loss and we'll be in demand at the pub quiz. As a former colleague of mine used to say, quoting (without knowing it) Sun Tzu, "time spent on reconnaissance is seldom wasted."[25]

In thinking about our change initiative, we have to know what's going on around us. We never know quite when those global forces we think aren't relevant to us could impact what we're trying to do. We're resourceful – so we can be aware and ready.

OUR OWN PRIVATE STONE AGE

While we're looking at the world in a particular way and lots of stuff is happening within it, our brain is often doing its own thing.

For every book or article that tells us we're hardwired to resist change, there's another that says the contrary. The success of humankind when compared to other species (realistically, our only benchmark unless Mulder was right),[26] many of whom had a healthy head start on us, strongly suggests the latter. We've come a long way in a short time in evolutionary terms.

There are areas, however, where our emotional and intellectual development has moved at a different pace from the evolution of our neural circuitry. In many respects we're still primitive. "You can take the person out of the Stone Age ... but you can't take the Stone Age out of the person."[27] For most of our time on the planet, we hunted animals in small groups to survive and at the same time tried to avoid being eaten, wholly or partially. Since the need to do so waned with the arrival, around 12,000 years ago, of agriculture and the beginning of settled communities we've instinctively learned to work with and around our Stone Age infrastructure.

There are some parts of our primitive brain that control change-related functions, little components with huge clout. Particularly important are those related to the release of serotonin and dopamine, discharging (or not) the feel-good reward-hungry gloop, the living embodiment of the 'like' button. Two tiny areas are especially important in this regard. The *amygdala* kicks in when we're threatened or scared, suppressing rational functionality so it can focus on the immediate threat – being eaten. Or being asked by leadership to do something we instinctively don't want to. The more-recently understood *habenula,* on the other hand, encodes information related to the disappointment from receiving smaller than expected rewards ("Is that all?" moments), rendering us apprehensive about failing. Even when we're told it's an essential feature of the creative process. Both have an impact on our attitudes to change that require us to understand that our body and, hence, our emotions, often react to success, threat and failure independently of our conscious thought.

We then have to contend with a feature that has ironically garnered much attention in the modern age, our increasing lack of attention. The proliferation of what can loosely (possibly generously) be described as 'content' delivered via hyper portable supercomputers (smartphones) has brought us the possibility of multitasking like never before. It's been shell shock for our cognitive evolution. The 'ability' to multitask may, however, just be illusory. We can only concentrate on one challenging task at once. Heavy media-multitaskers, however, far from proving their self-conferred superior status, are less able to filter the onslaught of irrelevance.[28] As Richard Seymour suggests, "The state of distraction we idealize as 'multitasking' is a form of squandering."[29] As some crave it, we might call it 'squanderlust.' As change leaders we'll be battling for the attention of our colleagues against a deluge of ever-scrolling temptation – not for actual information or matters of interest or tasks requiring action, but the rarely delivered *potential* for them. We're increasingly living in hope.

This type of neural activity is the stuff we can't do anything about even if we wanted to. Change projects often fall foul of thinking that a rationalized modern idea or construct can roll back three million years of genetically accumulated experience, most of which was significantly more existentially challenging than modern life. I recently listened to a very smart corporate leader confidently describe how he was going to "make people less territorial" as though it was a transactional arrangement. One thing we've successfully managed to iron out over many hundreds of generations is how tough it used to be out there, such that we actually believe we can do this kind of thing.

In thinking about our change initiative, we're not always rational, logical beings in full control of our own decision-making faculties. We can't forget that a significant part of us is still watching and waiting for a cloudless sky and a full moon.

OUR SCALE

While we're looking at the world in a particular way, lots of stuff is happening within it and our brain is doing its own thing, stuff we think should make sense doesn't seem to.

When contemplating the power and reach of macro forces, we're rather seduced by the notion of scalability. It's the basis of capitalism, perpetual growth. We think that when faced with certain challenging situations we simply need to do more to counter or unlock them. A directly proportional response.

However, the problems of form, scale and size are as intrinsic to the human-made world as they are to the natural.[30] Put simply, beasts, buildings and organizations can't get bigger without evolving into something else. This is the 'square–cube law,' first articulated by Galileo Galilei in 1638.

It can be stated as: "When an object undergoes a proportional increase in size, its new surface area is proportional to the square of the multiplier and its new volume is proportional to the cube of the multiplier."[31] That is, an object's mass cubes with a doubling of its size.

It's the same principle with leading change, and one that has baffled many a leader: it doesn't scale in the way we instinctively expect. It may not be quite as mathematically unequivocal or qualify as a 'law,' but generally when the size of our initiative doubles, its mass – the relationship between the issues and all those factors discussed in this chapter – cubes. There are more dependencies and interactions in the complex adaptive systems, more transformations, altered forms of resistance, a different evolutionary path. We can't always simply add proportionally more change resource to get us through. As in, more people, material, media and interventions. The initiative has evolved and become something different. It needs to be recognized as having changed, and our programme re-thought, re-planned and re-applied accordingly.

In thinking about our change initiative, as issues increase numerically, we can't always just proportionally apply more resources. We have to think and respond in cubes.

LOCAL THINKING

We're now at a human level – the things we think, applied to the organization we're within.

VALUES AND CONTEXT

Leading change needs reference to both the unique context in which it occurs (what we can and can't do), and the values that determine our actions (what we will and won't do). Both give meaning to what we think and understand and the course we take (or choose not to).

VALUES

Values are principles or standards we consider important. They govern our thought and action and tell us what, for us, is right and wrong. Sometimes values are conscious, in that we know what they are and can name and describe them; sometimes they operate unconsciously. If trust is a value, we don't go ahead and drop a colleague in trouble to advance our own agenda. Even if the opportunity presents itself as an open goal, they've previously done the same to us or we believe that on this occasion we won't get caught. We see values as a constant. They're reliable and reassuring in a chaotic world – and in the midst of a change initiative.

There are some hurdles with values.

First, they work on two levels – personal and organizational. We all have values to which we ascribe, and we bring them to the workplace. The organization's values are often worked out by a small and detached subset at a country club with robust coffee and cold towels and then everyone is asked to declare their agreement to those chosen values and act accordingly. Alignment between our own and the organization's values may have been a factor (in both directions) in our joining. Equally, they may have not even been considered during the process, leaving our values potentially misaligned or even conflicting with those of our colleagues or the organization – or both.

Second, interpretation of the meaning of values can vary. Rightly or wrongly, a value is usually expressed as a single word. Two people may both have the same declared value but see and understand it differently. If we value creativity, this could be just as easily interpreted as a love of paintings of oversized combs as it could to provide tacit consent to dubious outcome-oriented behaviour, avoiding policies and rules. Similarly, roles and their demands upon us vary. It's tough when we're in a statutory compliance role to be asked to challenge and disrupt. We need to take the value and collectively craft – and agree to – its meaning.

Third, values are important to us, but not always absolute. Honesty may be a value, but a circumstance may arise where a significant injustice may be prevented, or a cherished legend preserved, from telling a small fib that (we hope) no one will notice. We may take a utilitarian, 'greater good' view. Think of the Tooth Fairy or Santa Claus, neither of whom exist. Do they?

Finally, it's commonplace for organizational values to be painted on the office walls – and then ignored. They have to drive compatible behaviour, or they mean nothing. That's up to us all. Values aren't decoration, physically or metaphorically.

Despite the inherent challenges, values alignment, based on clear and unambiguous definitions, is a vital part of leading change. The more that what we want to achieve is compatible with what people will do, the greater our chance of success. Discovering the required common values and framing a change programme around them is an essential pre-initiative task, part of that reconnaissance that isn't wasted. It's not especially difficult. We can sketch them out – what the value is, a meaning we can agree upon, and a number of behaviours against each that will demonstrate it. An example is given in Table 2. We can try starting with our own, filling in the blank lines and adding more as we need. Albeit if we exceed five or six, we may find the process (and living up to them) a little onerous.

VALUE	MEANING (WE AGREE ON)	BEHAVIOUR THAT WILL ILLUSTRATE IT
EMPOWERMENT	When faced with challenges we give our people the freedom to develop solutions, guiding and offering support as needed	• Regular scheduled one-to-ones with our team members to review tasks and offer guidance • Visible support for a solution developed by a team member • Understanding and securing the resources our team need to be successful
VALUE 2		
VALUE 3		
VALUE 4		
VALUE 5		

TABLE 2

CONTEXT

Our context is the combination of the background, environment and circumstances in which we'll lead change. It has components, including (but not limited to) structure, history, stories, physical environment, processes, rules and laws, policies, people, relationships, attitudes, norms and leadership. It shapes the meaning in all communication, engagement and activity. Everything that happens is interpreted through it. It's another filter below our world view.

With values – being a question of willingness or preparedness to act informed by principles, conscience, morality or belief – action is allowed or prohibited *by us*. We could do it, and it's permitted, we just don't believe it's right. With context, given that it's comprised of components to which we're subject but of which we're not necessarily in control, action is allowed or prohibited by factors *other than us*. Some things we can't do even if we wanted to. Without, say, breaking the rules.

There are three other considerations with context.

First, it's always unique. The somewhat groan-worthy expression that greets every traveller – "it's different here" – is actually true. It doesn't imply a degree. We just shouldn't be so ready to feed the assertion. That's because it's true of everywhere and not just the location in which the claim is made. It's even true in the same place at a different time. It's why what worked last time *may not* work this time. Butterflies have flapped, the complex systems have adapted and evolved.

Second, it's always dynamic. As much as this book is intended to generate confidence in applying a tried-and-tested approach, there's no such thing as a context-free route to successful change, a pure laboratory-tested and uncontaminated objective path. We can't ride roughshod over context. Fortune may favour the brave but not the daft. We also need to be cognizant of the fact that our initiative is impacting it and changing it as we act. We're as much a part of it as anyone else.

Finally, while context is vitally important, it's not necessarily *everything*. There are two reasons. First, we can seek to understand its limitations and opportunities, and work with it and around it. Where it appears prohibitive, such as with the generic corporate 'fault lines' we cover in Part Two (technology, process, activity and communication), as it's comprised of loosely associated components we can often weave a way through, playing some off against the others. There will be opportunities if we look far enough ahead or are suitably creative. Second, we should also recognize that there may be aspects of context of which we won't be aware, or won't be able to see through our lens, and therefore won't be able to grasp or work with. These hidden or invisible aspects may leave us forever wondering why things happened the way they did.

For the purposes of leading change, a relationship exists between values and context that gives us the opportunity to target our planning (Figure 10).

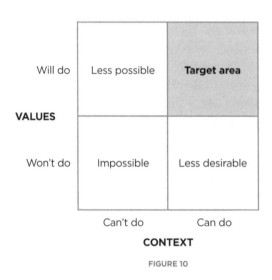

FIGURE 10

We have a clear sweet spot – things that are *possible* that people *will do*. It means there are three other quadrants where getting anything done may be problematic. We either have to attend to circumstances (time and probably money) or people (time, understanding and consideration). Or we have to do something different. It's quite likely, however, that in operating in the target area we can create opportunities to make inroads into the other quadrants as they're not mutually exclusive for all time.

On joining a large multinational organization, my first change initiative was in a Central European country that hadn't long emerged from Soviet control. Believing that corporate involvement, bringing expertise and experience to the project, would be welcomed, I approached the challenge logically. I used what I considered to be tried-and-tested methods. They didn't work. At one early meeting myself and a colleague were clearly being sworn at in a guttural rendition of the native tongue by over a dozen angry local managers. My colleague leaned across and whispered to me, "I don't think this is going very well." I had misunderstood local sentiment, norms and practices and had to quickly adapt my approach to align both with their values and the context. The early experience was invaluable, if a little painful.

In thinking about our change initiative, we must first identify and operate where people can and will act. It makes other change possible.

MAKING STUFF HAPPEN: MANAGING AND LEADING

As we're establishing, change is messy. Unlike the natural world, where evolution runs its course through transformations, reproduction and luck, unencumbered by time constraints, in the corporate world we don't have that luxury. It calls for both management and leadership. Put the 'right' people in charge, and it should all happen swimmingly. If only that really were the case.

We referred to managers and leaders as actors in our change initiative in the Opening Gambit, and we'll consider leadership specifically more fully in Part Two. Here we're concerned with both at a more conceptual level.

Plenty is written by others about managing and leading, with the former usually coming off far worse. Managers appear to be an easier target. They have the unenviable job of creating and maintaining confidence through controlled progress.

Success is the expected outcome. Anything less is unacceptable. Their title is usually given and agreed, accompanying and to a degree describing their role. The criteria for their success are usually many and are often defined in terms of clear(ish) metrics. They often have to provide options for leadership and rationalize their actions and decisions. When answers are needed, they're supposed to work them out. Loyalty has to be earned. When organizations need to cut costs, reinvigorate or repurpose themselves, they usually shed managers first, as though it was a complete surprise there were so many hiding in plain sight. In the arcane middle, that is. A failure in a role is likely to necessitate a step down the career ladder in order to rebuild lost credibility.

Leaders, on the other hand, are expected to motivate, inspire, instil action in others, and to unblock the path where needed. Success is the hoped-for outcome, but with an appreciation that a whole variety of factors may prevent it. They usually have a formal role title but are informally referred to as, or claim to be, a 'leader.' The criteria for success are usually far more limited. They're supposed to have all the answers. Loyalty is expected, a natural response. Character is often seen as more important than skill or experience – and just as likely to be the reason for their downfall, too. It's from this that often stems myth, the *idea* of the leader rather than the reality. On occasions the two are aligned. Failure isn't always a career impediment. Sometimes it can even be an advantage if the manner of the failure was considered heroic (as per the myth) or the odds deemed unfavourably stacked. Or both.

The roles are rarely discrete, however. Managers are often leaders of something, and leaders still usually have to manage something. It's probably more the case in the 21st century organization that leaders have to be responsible managers, too. It can't be all table thumping and over-the-cliff-we-go bravado, as at some point this usually ends at the bottom of the cliff.

It's often held that management is something we can coach and develop, whereas leadership is innate, born out of a *need* to lead. That is, we *train* managers and *find* leaders. That's not necessarily true, of course, as the emergence of an entire leadership development industry suggests. Essentially, with both management and leadership, as with many skills, a kernel of ability and potential is regarded as a vital starting point, and the rest can be learned.[32] The precise proportion of each required has been difficult to pin down.

Common to both managers and leaders is **authority** (the *right* to do something), which is usually conferred by a formal position, and **power** (the *capacity* to do it), which is *sometimes* conferred by a position, but at other times simply assumed or seized. They're related, and in most cases accompany one another, but are all too often confused.

We can have power without authority. This lacks formal legitimacy and is often associated with political upheaval where the leaders derive a power from the trust and support of their followers. Likewise, we can have authority without power, which isn't much use at all. When team sports managers 'lose the dressing room,' players cease to listen to instruction from, or follow the commands of, the one with the initials on their tracksuit.

Power and authority don't always have to be proportional, either. Sometimes relatively junior figures can wield extraordinary power. Think Derek 'Red Robbo' (as the UK press nicknamed him) Robinson, tormentor of British Leyland in the 1970s, a trade union convenor who led a staggering 523 walkouts over less than three years at the firm's Longbridge Plant in Birmingham.[33] Similarly, relatively senior figures can be hamstrung by process or procedure. 'Lame duck' political leaders are those serving out their time having not been re-elected or having lost their eligibility for office.

Table 3 provides a quick recap of the commonly perceived differences:

	LEADERS	MANAGERS
QUANTITY	Few	Many
TITLE	Claimed	Conferred
SUCCESS CRITERIA	Few	Many
DATA POINTS	Few	Many
KEY ROLE	Motivation	Control
GENERAL PERCEPTION	Positive	Negative
PERCEPTION OF ORIGIN	Born	Made
KEY ATTRIBUTE	Character	Skills
CAREER TIMELINE	Variable	Long
EXPERIENCE	Preferred	Required
AUTHORITY	Preferred	Required
POWER	Required	Preferred

TABLE 3

A change initiative needs to be both led and managed. That is, galvanized (to identify and pursue the opportunity) and controlled (to plan and resource, and to prepare for uncertainty). Yet in corporate parlance the most commonly used expression is 'change management.' This is perhaps to reinforce change as a tactical discipline (at best), or to emphasize the importance of control. We could spend inordinate amounts of time and energy contesting this, but we're probably better served by understanding the differences and the necessary contribution that leaders and managers make and ensuring that our initiative is resourced accordingly.

It should, at this stage, be noted that **sponsorship** isn't akin to leadership. Sponsors lend their name to an initiative for legitimacy and validation. Almost every change initiative needs and has them. They offer protection. As sponsorship is about visible and recognizable support, not action, it generally doesn't involve any specific contribution to the initiative. Similarly, if we're a sponsor, we're not expecting to offer any. When we're asked to sponsor someone's cycle ride for charity, the rider doesn't expect to see us alongside them in awkwardly stretchy gear at the start line.

In thinking about our change initiative, managers need leaders and leaders need managers: we should be careful not to prize one over the other. And at some stage, for the benefit of both, we'll need to secure sponsorship.

MAKING STUFF HAPPEN: INFLUENCING AND ENABLING

Making stuff happen needs both formal and specifically assigned roles (management, leadership and governance, for example) and informal opportunities to create a difference, such as influencing and enabling. The formally assigned are relatively few in number. The informal encompass us all, including those formally appointed.

Influencing is being able to have an effect on others without the possession or exercise of any formal authority. We must *do something* to create influence. It can generate empathy, impact and movement in others without any visible sign of compulsion. We influence via action that can be verbal, emotional or physical, and we do it in some small way simply by being present. We make something happen without having *appeared* to have asked or instructed anyone to do anything.

As such, we can all influence change, regardless of where we rank in the corporate shakedown. It's often a competency required in any mid-level-and-above job role. As such, it can be interpreted as an admission that organizational processes and structures could be better. It's no surprise that in a social-media-infused world it's become a role in its own right. As a result, all the naffest social-platform biographies include a claim to be an influencer. For some, however, it's a lucrative job, channelling sponsorship and preferred status, feeding in each case a hungry, willing and impatient audience of millions.

Whereas influencing invites something to happen, **enabling** makes something possible. It can be active in that we do something specific and identifiable to allow something to happen, or passive in that we don't get in the way of something happening, and thereby give consent. The latter can sometimes be unconscious – by removing ourselves, we can give the impression to others that we've consented. This is then all too often followed by a backtracking of "I didn't mean ..."

Empowerment (contender for buzzword of the 21st century, so far) is one form of enabling. It's the granting of the right (authority) or means (power) to others to think, feel or do something.

We can at this point bring all four ideas together – the formal (management and leadership) and the informal (influencing and enabling) – and express them in terms of the actions resulting at the intersection of each to help understand the relationships. We can also start with the terms within the panes of Figure 11 and read out to what processes are bringing them about (as in, if we're planning, then it's likely we're managing in a formal sense and enabling in an informal).

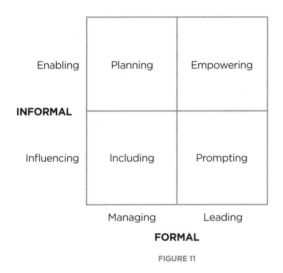

FIGURE 11

The reality is that all four are usually happening simultaneously, some intended and some not, and often in different directions. As we've established, nothing stands still.

It's also worth considering that with the possibilities for action and inaction, conscious and unconscious, on the part of everyone within the sphere of our change initiative, it's almost impossible for anyone not to have a role, however small.

In thinking about our change initiative, we must be leaders, managers, enablers and influencers of change. We should know and recognize the difference and pursue and deploy each appropriately.

INERTIA, RESISTANCE AND COMPLACENCY

Change initiatives almost always find opposition. Lumping it all together as a generic problem isn't helpful in understanding or dealing with it. Essentially, there are three types: inertia, resistance and complacency.

Change initiatives are always a move away from the default. The default has enormous power. It's what we're doing now, the way things are. In what's called 'choice architecture' (the way we structure and frame choices), the three key considerations in how people decide are: the presence of a default, the range of alternatives and how each alternative is described. We're more likely to choose the default, unless there's an imperative that suggests it's an unsustainable option, or a matter of compliance that leaves no choice. Yet, in respect of our initiative, it's not our chosen path. If we assume that we're choice-making creatures and that free will isn't some kind of illusory overlay to a predetermined universe, there's something significant here for leading change.

We need to distinguish clearly between inertia, the *passive* tendency not to change speed or direction (avoiding doing something), and resistance, the *active* opposition to movement (pushing back against something).

Inertia is an unconscious attribute of nature. It depicts the potential of a moving object not to be deflected from its straight path and constant speed when something gets in the way. It keeps still things still, and moving things moving. In human terms we think of it as doing nothing different.

Unless we're an antsy tinkerer or a serial rebel, we'll keep doing what we're doing until something happens. In change terms, inertia will be present regardless, given the way that adaptation and evolution work. Even in change initiatives where there's little active opposition there's always a degree of inertia.

Our task is to minimize the impact of inertia, but not to remove it altogether. Sometimes it's useful as it creates the necessary time for consideration and evaluation. We may have got something wrong in our idea, assumptions, communication or engagement. It can be likened to another party proofreading what we've been working on solidly for a long time and finding errors we've missed because we're so familiar with the text. We wouldn't spot a typo if it was in Wingdings. As I experienced when writing this book.

Resistance, however, is a conscious application of a force to a moving object to try to stop or deflect it. It doesn't always wear a T-shirt proclaiming its identity. We often mistakenly ascribe naturally occurring, non-disruptive inertia such as contemplation or learning to this category, where nothing *appears* to be happening despite our requests. Understanding the difference is therefore vital.

The character and nature of resistance can be complex. It can range from the passive (stubbornness, refusal) to the active (sabotage), and from the individual, random and spontaneous to the organized, specific and targeted. It can be rational or emotional, proactive or reactive. It can be wholesale or detailed and specific. It can be a combination of all of these factors over time.

When we're subject to a change initiative, our values, both as they relate to ourselves and the organization, play a key role in determining whether we resort to resistance. If we do, we may find ourselves in a minority, with others happy to acquiesce. We're forced to make a decision.

Sometimes it's simply that matters from our personal life find an outlet in what's happening in our professional. We transfer the frustration and anger felt in our own space to something over which we feel we may have more control, that appears more tangible. When a colleague takes umbridge at a proposed change and the reaction appears to be disproportional, there is often something else unrelated going on.

I once received an email from a senior colleague who had arrived at our office in London early in the morning on an overnight flight from the USA. It was sent at around 7am. The initial few lines were a complaint that the office café did not stock his preferred brand of soda. From there, the remainder of the full A4 page of closely typed text became a progressively frustrated rant about my causal role in everything that wasn't right in his world. There wasn't just something, there was a whole lot else going on.

Whether it's an individual or collective act, planned or spontaneous, resistance isn't of itself helpful. We instinctively want to counter it, so we devote disproportionate time and energy to doing so. We get drawn in and find that getting out again is extremely difficult. Some of our behaviours as leaders of the initiative can perpetuate the intent to resist. Positions polarize and solidify. Chief among them are not listening or listening and not responding, and the use of language indicative of confrontation.

However, the strength of feeling and the causes that generate resistance need to be understood. The resistors may be those who care enough to act. They may see or feel things in ways we haven't. They are potentially therefore a treasure trove of insight. Our response should be inquisitive in the first instance and proportionate thereafter. Our goal is never 100% support for our initiative because if we make it so, it'll torment and unbalance us. However compelling we feel our case to be, we can't pretend there won't be a degree of resistance. Sometimes simply allowing more space and time is enough.

We also need to note that inertia and resistance aren't the same as **complacency**, a contented yet often misguided satisfaction with the way things are seen to be. At the harsh end of the scale it's self-delusion, the creation of a false reality. It's considered and deliberate, and not only is it not part of the learning process, it's a prohibitor. It prevents listening, engagement and involvement, as there is deemed to be no need of any. As it results from a considered choice, we can regard it as a form of resistance. However, it's much easier dealing with those who openly resist and are able to express why than with those who simply shut us out. While we often deal with change at an emotional level, complacency needs to be met head-on with dry and compelling evidence. It may in time help us to strike a chord.

In thinking about our change initiative, we need to watch carefully for the difference between inertia, resistance and complacency. We must understand the type of fire before choosing the extinguisher. Some just make it worse. We should remember, too, that we can't assume we can scale our response when any of these factors increase.

FAIRNESS

As a significant contribution to minimizing resistance, change needs to be fair.

That isn't an idealistic assertion, and it doesn't necessarily mean it should be evenly distributed. The initiative may affect some people more than others but can still be led in a fair manner – equitably, impartially and without discrimination.

The 'platform-burners' may tell us at this stage that fairness has nothing to do with it if there's an imperative, real or manufactured. Yet fairness is both known and – even more powerfully – felt. The sense of not being treated fairly is likely to be harboured and resurface at any given time, possibly many times. It hardens into resentment.

If we're on the receiving end of, or witness to, unfairness, we're likely to do something about it to try and right the situation.

It may manifest in the most subtle forms of resistance. As human beings, we're remarkably resourceful and will fathom any kind of workaround that suits if we don't think we've been treated even-handedly. This is often concluded at a management level to be 'old habits' refusing to budge or resurfacing, but the seeds are often sown at a very early stage and will frame all future interactions. Once planted, they're hard to dig up.

Fairness, as an aspiration and a standard, is rarely entirely objective. It's a test we have to devise and apply, and after consideration, be happy it's been met. As such, it's often best not handled alone and should be regularly revisited.

SHORTCUTS

Our final reflections here reduce us to the most local thinking of all – ourselves.

Sometimes whatever we say or do, people will do their own thing regardless. 'Desire lines' are usually the shortest and easiest path between two points. The idea is essentially taken from the natural world, in the trails forged by migrating animals. For us, despite 'keep to the path' notices in many landscaped or parkland areas, if the given walkways are two sides of a square and we're heading from A to C, we'll skip B and find a trail across the diagonal, the shortest route (Figure 12). We may need to trample the foliage to do so, but soon others will follow.

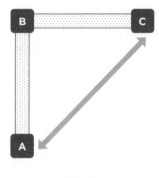

FIGURE 12

Desire lines are a source of much fascination. While in the natural world (as far as we know, of course) they're matters of pure expediency, for us they can be the exercise of personal control, a conscious rebellion with limited consequences yet inflated with satisfaction.

Interestingly, just as their creation results from an initial act of free will on the part of one person subsequently repeated by others, once created, desire lines tend to generate an informal compliance of their own. The rebellion slowly solidifies into the establishment. We rarely step off the strips we've worn, perhaps because they're the shortest route, but possibly because they seem made by *us* rather than an authority, as though we've had some part in it.

In our sense, the idea of desire lines is metaphorical. This type of behaviour is mirrored in non-physical settings and scenarios, where we take the easiest path regardless of the instruction. We devise workarounds, ways of moving from A to C without passing through B. They often conflict with the 'official' process. With the universal, global and local influences on change at play, we should never underestimate the human being's willingness to softly rebel.

We can, of course, harness this spirit through a perpetual beta mindset. The Dutch architect Rem Koolhaas did just this at the Illinois Institute of Technology campus in the 1990s by not creating any paths at all on the campus.[34] He waited for the students to tread the routes they wanted to take, after which the worn lines were paved. He turned the tendency to rebel after the fact into co-creation, at the initial cost of a few muddy shoes. Not his, of course.

Similarly, many of the most trodden paths in our urban environments today were once forged as expedient routes long before. One such is Broadway in New York, an original desire line called the Wickquasgeck Path formed by the Native Americans.

Interestingly, many new desire lines have appeared during the Covid-19 pandemic. Instead of taking us along the shortest route between two points, they've often extended our path as we've sought physical distance from one another, snaking away from paved paths through tall grasses. They've become less an act of rebellion, more one of self-preservation. They'll likely grow over as the need subsides.

In thinking about our change initiative, where the desire lines already exist, the solution we're seeking may, too. Where the problem is new, we need to find and work to the shortest paths – and take the first steps ourselves.

PART ONE WRAP

The summaries at the end of each part of the book are intended to be takeaway one-liners. Here are a few points to reflect on from Part One:

- Change isn't *a thing*, it's part of us. It's our essence.
- Change never starts and stops – the only bookends are those we helpfully apply. We're forever in *perpetual beta*, never finished, always creating, together.
- When we think something has started, it already has. When we think something has finished, it's becoming something else.
- Evolution comprises many transformations. And a little luck.
- We don't change people, they change themselves. We provide what's needed for them to adapt. Sometimes in doing so they change us.
- Change needs managers as much as it needs leaders. They're like oars. Just one or the other won't get us anywhere but around in circles.
- We all influence and enable change. We're never bystanders.
- We're operating in the right zone when enabled by context (what we can do) and values (what we will do).
- Change can be impacted by inertia, resistance and complacency. We need to listen, extract the insight, let some of it go, and manage the rest.
- To take the easiest route is to be human. Leaders sometimes need to follow the path already worn.

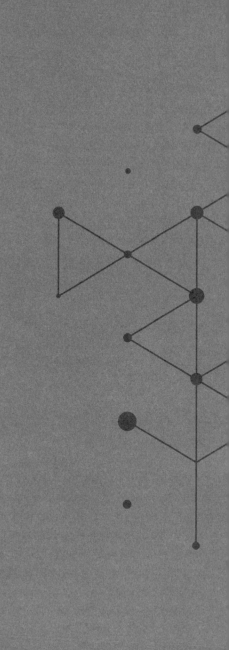

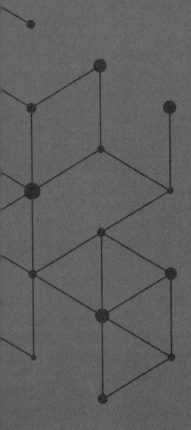

PREPARATION
HOW ARE WE GOING TO DO IT?

THE OPERATING SYSTEM
OF CHANGE

Ideas don't always become change initiatives. One of five things usually happen to each – rejected, forgotten, saved for later (consciously or unconsciously), modified or acted on. When acted on, most of the time what's needed just gets done, with minimal planning and enough conviction and commitment to see it through. Change simply occurs, sometimes with a little guidance.

Very often this is regarded as 'continuous improvement.' This is something almost everyone at any level of the organization is expected to undertake. That is, always looking for ways to improve methods, processes or outputs to make them better against a range of measures (cost, speed, efficiency, quality and accuracy among others). This type of change is embedded in everyday working life, its identification and implementation absorbed without breaking stride.

The only characteristic qualifying an idea as 'change' is that something will be different at the other end from the way it is today. Yet at some undefined point we *may* elect that it qualifies, and so we decide we must do something about it. Who actually decides is an important consideration. Ideas are funnelled within organizations into a power structure that's fundamentally political. We'll need to assume there's a workable process and a set of criteria, however flexible. It could be the scale (size or reach) that qualifies it, the distance we're asking people to move, the investment in systems or processes, the implications of the idea on other parts of the organization, the dependencies involved, the likely benefit (profit, market share or status) or just the sheer excitement of it. There are no universal or objective rules to which we can refer: either we decide, or someone decides for us.

Sometimes it's not even considered to be an initiative worthy of its salt without a name being assigned, often randomized to protect its purpose. This naturally often satisfies those we identified in Part One as seeing change as a conspiracy. Fundamentally, however, at this juncture, our act needs to come together. The operating system of change is how we make this happen.

WHY A CHANGE OPERATING SYSTEM?

Why can't we just go from an understanding of change (Part One) to doing some change stuff (Part Three) and skip all of this? Why can't we just get it done? The answer is simply that we're actually considering all of what we shall describe as the components of our operating system, even if we're not aware of some (or all) of them. What we're doing here is exploring how with conscious consideration we might do it better and more thoroughly to create an improved chance of success.

We're used to the term 'operating system,' principally because the devices that power our lives all have them. It's the most important software that runs on a computer. It manages the computer's memory and processes, as well as all of its software and hardware. It also allows us to communicate with the computer without knowing how to speak the computer's language, which is handy as the vast majority of us don't and wouldn't want to learn anyway (I know this because I once had to take a course in assembly language programming). It runs everything and everything runs on it. It's quite simple as to what would happen to the machine without it – absolutely nothing.

The glory, however, usually goes to the applications, the stuff we use. They're identifiable, they have cool names and icons, and we talk about them. When we consider what has changed our own lives, we refer to them. What we want from the operating system, meanwhile, is slick, smooth and fast running, a barely discernible purr. It's of a particular genre of system that we notice primarily when it *doesn't* work.

We mentioned in Part One that our operating system was concerned with the *how* of change. We *could* just move from thinking about change to doing lots of things, but we won't be prepared or ready, so we won't be able to do the stuff we think we can. We'll have our own equivalent of a box full of useless stuff.

COMPONENTS OF THE OPERATING SYSTEM

There are six components of the operating system:

- Opportunity: seeing what's possible, however ambitious or challenging, therefore often prompting and certainly always enabling the change initiative
- Vision: homing in on what we wish to achieve and capturing it succinctly
- Evidence: bringing the possible to life, thereby proving its viability
- Leadership: making the possible happen, delivering it
- Trust: securing the opportunity, such that we all believe it's possible
- Resources: making the possible *possible*, and enabling it

We can show the operating system graphically as per Figure 13:

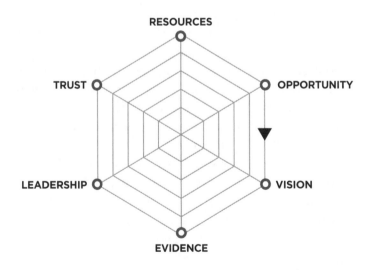

FIGURE 13

The 'spider' (or radar) chart is a handy tool[35] as it helps us to reinforce the interrelationships between the components. It aids recall, and ensures that as we consider each component, we do so with reference to the others to avoid duplication or omission. We can therefore use it to monitor progress and development.

PRINCIPLES OF THE OPERATING SYSTEM

There are five underlying principles of the operating system.

It's considered that each of the six components will be present to some degree in any change initiative. This is the first principle – **universality**. The components may vary in scale or contribution, but they're always there.

Second, the operating system has **structure**. An operating system has an architecture, a means of organizing its components to ensure that it works and can be developed. Each is related both to the others and to the whole. They're not a list, or a random assemblage of good things to have. The structure has meaning and purpose.

Third, given its structure – the intrinsic relationship between each component – it's capable of supporting **measurement**, either quantitative or qualitative. In this way it actually reinforces one of the components – evidence. We'll have a look at this when we've explored each of the components.

Fourth, it's **open source**. Anyone can contribute and share; in fact, it's positively encouraged. It's hoped that this description kick-starts the development of a universal, structured and rich body of work around enabling change. Much of what already exists – and there's plenty – might be organized in this way. While I've set it out here, it doesn't make me the authority on it by any means. Just as our devices continually receive upgrades and fixes, consider this offering to be version 1.0. From here, we can all contribute.

Lastly, it's **usable**. It can be deployed from the earliest flicker of change through to beyond the achievement of the vision, from planning tool to active tracker of success. Or, as Professor Piehead would say, of partial success. Unlike a simple to-do list, bullet-point arrangement or acronym, the relationships illustrated ensure thoroughness.

From here we shall consider each component in turn. While this is a system that's itself in a state of perpetual motion, our first point of entry with our change initiative is the opportunity. All else flows from this opening and, in time, will modify it.

OPPORTUNITY

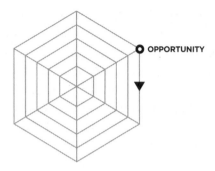

An opportunity is a moment or set of circumstances that makes it possible to do something. For change to happen, there has to be an opportunity. It's the space we're intending to move into, the gap between now and a future state. As nothing stands still, the space will last for only a limited and often unknowable time. It's not only our natural starting point, but it's very often the starting point that occurred before we even identified it. We usually 'take' or 'seize' an opportunity, implying possession. We bring it to us. So, we have to recognize, understand, evaluate and plan for it before we do anything else. And in doing so, if we believe it to be worthwhile, make sure we don't miss it.

There are two ways to identify the opportunity. It may exist and make itself known in some way. In this respect we may notice it or someone may bring it to our attention. That could mean anything, including an evident process failure, a repeatedly missed target, a gap in the market, or something specifically posted such as an advertised job opening (usually conveniently called an 'opportunity'). Time in this instance will be a critical factor. Or, there may be something we wish to do to create it through a series of preceding 'if–then' steps, like gaining a particular qualification so as to be eligible for such a career opportunity. In such instances we're more concerned with timing than time per se. Either way, we've seen something ahead.

We identify the opportunity in a much broader, more granular way than a vision, sometimes even as a story. A sketch of where we wish to get to contains narrative, explanation and analysis. It encapsulates an understanding of the history (or at least our best interpretation) of how we arrived at the present, what's happening (or not) now and a desired future. It opens a channel of uncertainty and ambiguity. We create less stability by decoupling the present and future. We stimulate the complex adaptive systems, as we covered in Part One.

OPPORTUNITY MAPPING

We may capture all of this as an opportunity map, to ensure through excitement or ambition we're not leaping into an abyss of our own making. It helps our team as exists so far into a common place and forms the outline of an organizational proposal. We can do so by looking at the past, present and desired future against a number of criteria. I've included some suggestions in Table 4, but the list isn't exhaustive, and may in some instances be too long. Clearly, if time is pressing we may have to do this on the fly.

	PAST	PRESENT	DESIRED FUTURE
ACTIVITY			
CONTEXT			
BROADER ENVIRONMENT			
PEOPLE			
PROCESSES			
KEY RELATIONSHIPS			
KEY INTERFACES			
KEY DEPENDENCIES			
TIME CONSIDERATIONS			
RESOURCES			
TECHNOLOGY/ SYSTEMS			
RISK AREAS			

TABLE 4

In terms of the past, there's always a reason for things being the way they are, despite the often-heard protestations of "How on earth did this happen?" Which is often followed by "This isn't a blame culture, but I want to know who was responsible." Someone somewhere thought it was a good idea at the time or the right way to do it. There will probably have been broader circumstances the audit trail is unable to reveal. Fortune, misfortune, coincidence or a change of priorities may have had a hand in it since, but there was an intent and often a design. Discovering the history isn't always easy in larger organizations. Very often the knowledge of a situation or decision walks out of the door with the individual concerned. That said, we need to try to understand how we got here.

Our present should be the easiest part to capture and needs little clarification. Unless, of course, we're playing with our phone and not paying attention. Our desired future at this stage is a scene-painting exercise. It's loose, with much of the detail missing. It helps for us to think about it in structured terms. It's important to enrich it, too – how it looks, feels and sounds.

KNOW, THINK, HOPE

We can think about our desired future in three ways, as seen in Figure 14.

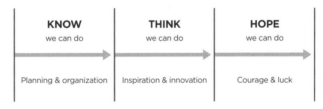

KNOW	THINK	HOPE
we can do	we can do	we can do
Planning & organization	Inspiration & innovation	Courage & luck

FIGURE 14

First, things we **know** we can do. Those that are within reach, that if we just divert our attention from day-to-day activities, we **can** achieve with planning and organization and with the operating system of change described here. There may still be associated risks but they're more procedural, or susceptible to the odd guerrilla activity from those with a competing agenda or sense of mischief.

Second, things we **think** we can do. Those that with a little more galvanizing of colleagues, pitching for resources and some non-linear thinking we **could** achieve.

Third, things we **hope** we can do. Those that are a long shot. They're stretch goals or whatever corporate adage works for challenges that we **might** achieve, that seem to lie beyond the possible but not yet at the impossible as it presently stands, with what's known today. They require other things to change (those we know and think we can do) to become reality.

The breakdown of the opportunity may be as simple as a sales target: knowing that one figure is in reach, that another may be possible with more effort and creative thinking, and that with fair winds, planetary alignment and the competition all looking in the other direction a hoped-for target may be reached.

FIGURE 15

The reality is that this isn't the linear process of Figure 14, but one that looks more like the diagram shown in Figure 15. As we accomplish (or plan for) things we know we can do, they'll open the opportunities initially believed to be too difficult to attain. As with all aspects of change, they're iterative, they accumulate and evolve. The opportunity we initially capture doesn't have to be the finished article – there will still be much to discover.

OPPORTUNITY AND RISK

In reality the opportunity we initially identify is often many related opportunities. Each opportunity also has a correlating risk, as we briefly referenced in Part One. Two sides of the same thing. We might achieve x but there's a risk of y happening when we try. We're asking the optimists and pessimists to look at the same thing from entirely different sides.

The last line item on our opportunity map in Table 4 is a segue to another level of analysis. We'll first look at how we assess risk, as this is a more familiar model, and then apply it back to opportunity.

For all the preparedness, flexibility and planning undertaken, for the reasons explored so far in this book, stuff will go wrong. We must anticipate what might happen, and plan to mitigate it. We can spend a lifetime on it if we're not careful, but then we won't eat. Or we could, instead, be too blasé and believe the forces are with us, only to then get eaten. Either way and we're just choosing which unpalatable exit.

A straightforward, established and tested method of considering risk is to think through all possible negative outcomes in terms of frequency (of being exposed to the risk), likelihood (of it happening) and severity (how bad it could be if it does happen). We've already started thinking about and exploring two areas from Part One – the wider operating landscape and intrinsic problems within organizations. We have our head start.

First, we identify every possible risk, then score each accordingly. The scoring is usually a matter of judgment but allows for quantitative measures if available:

- Frequency – of the activity that gives rise to the risk (score out of 5)
- Likelihood – of it happening under normal circumstances (out of 5)
- Severity – if it were to happen (out of 10)

Given that severity is the existential consideration, it deserves a double weighting. Add them together and create a risk score (Table 5). When the key risks are assessed, we determine a threshold (our judgment call) above which we'll consider them worthy of detailed planning and resource allocation. We'll be able to assess where that threshold lies when we've set them out.

DESCRIPTION	FREQUENCY (5)	LIKELIHOOD (5)	SEVERITY (10)	TOTAL
Unavailability of raw materials	4	3	7	14
Political instability at source	2	4	9	15
Adverse weather	2	3	6	11
Risk 4				
Risk 5				

TABLE 5

We need to keep it soft and live, as the risks will change as the initiative progresses.

We can run the exercise in a similar fashion for opportunity (Table 6). We just replace 'severity' with 'impact' for the double-score. Assessing opportunities keeps the risks in perspective and ensures optimism is ever-present. It balances a mindset that's usually corporately loaded towards managing risk – of the reasons for *not* doing something. Again, we set a threshold at which planning and resource will be applied, so the opportunity is maximized. We similarly need to keep it flexible and live too.

DESCRIPTION	FREQUENCY (5)	LIKELIHOOD (5)	IMPACT (10)	TOTAL
Reduced production costs	5	4	9	18
Positive consumer ratings	4	5	7	16
New sales channels	3	3	8	14
Opportunity 4				
Opportunity 5				

TABLE 6

We'll explore the vision in the next chapter, but suffice to know for now, each opportunity should roll up to the vision. If we identify a super opportunity that doesn't, is the vision right? If we believe we might significantly reduce our carbon footprint as a result of our initiative and we'll focus attention on this aspect, it's probable that our vision ought to include it. The exercise is therefore a double-check on the validity of the vision.

THE SIZE OF THE ASK

Change is still the last frontier of many organizational disciplines. When overcomplicated and misunderstood, it's unduly reliant on the actual outcome as the hopeful key: "You'll love it, so you'll get it." Which is often: "*We* love it, so you'll get it." While identifying our opportunity we have a significant chance to consider how far we're asking our colleagues to move.

Our case for the change is often coherent, logical and emotional. Even romantic. It may be something our colleagues want to do; might want to do but haven't yet become aware of or rationalized; or will want to do, however unwelcome when compared to a less palatable alternative that isn't yet known. The advantages may be beautifully balanced between the qualitative and quantitative. The opportunity may be compelling and realistic, however ambitious. The intention may be airtight, watertight and, well, tight. All that's needed when it's all designed is for someone to 'do the change.'

It may appear to be an obvious consideration in regard to our opportunity but a necessary one – how big is the ask? As in, what's the distance we're asking people to move mentally and emotionally (and sometimes physically, too)? It needs a dispassionate and rational response. This is often difficult for those wholly vested in – and convinced by – the change. We're asking the people for whom the change is easiest, and in whom the idea is already firmly embedded, to determine how easy it'll be for those for whom potentially it's not and who'll be most affected.

It's at this point that decision bias is at its strongest. A collective feeling emerges among the initiative team that genuine concerns are merely the last twitches of blinkered resistance that will eventually play themselves out, exhausted. That any remaining anxiety can be squeezed out of significance. The air-punching inclination to 'be bold' can be infectious yet mask many awkward realities.

For the change to work, the underlying assumption is that people will have to do things or behave differently. The risk, however, is that our idea is only ever likely to be compelling to us, in abstract, given the size of the ask in reality.

As our opportunity is revealed, indicators of anxiety from those affected by the change mean that an emotional connection is being made, and that isn't prima facie a bad thing. It's not our job to remove it, but to understand it and decouple it from negativity. The manner in which it's expressed, as signals and clues, in the form of communication (direct and indirect) and behaviour, is the surest measure of the delta between *our* honest assessment of the size of the ask and that undertaken by those being asked to change.

The resolution lies in the fact that change is simultaneously pushed and pulled. Perhaps a little like a dance.

Pushed, as in proposed and justified, a case made for it, usually at a higher level in the body concerned, or from an external source. Pushed change has often been rationalized and assessed long before it's made known. Pushing, however, is harder than pulling due to the level of friction. In this case the friction comes from the source of the energy, the top-down nature of the initiative.

Pulled, as in requested or demanded, even if its specific form or detail is at that time missing, often from a more junior level or a less enfranchised quarter. Pulled change is often less formed and rationalized and is, instead, more emotional. It may also have been felt long before being expressed.

All of one and little of the other will mean heightened anxiety. Our opportunity needs to create the conditions for both push and pull. Far from negating them, turning one into the other, balancing the forces, doubles their impact. That is, turning a suggestion from the 'shop floor' into a management initiative, or creating a popular groundswell for change from leadership vision. It's where the size of the ask is understood, managed and converted into a positive intent, and where the opportunity appears at its most realizable. It requires early testing. This is often best conducted in a small, closed group entirely new to the idea, from different areas of the organization. There is no reason for us to prompt the denial and anger from the Kübler-Ross curve we outlined in the Opening Gambit.

We're readying ourselves so, at this stage, there's still time to recalibrate, review or reset the size of the ask. Perhaps we may break it down into more discrete, definable and digestible steps. Doing so isn't a defeat or a failure, nor does it equate to a loss of courage. Change can still be, and feel, bold. However, the moment it feels macho, our judgment has been clouded and it's time to step back. Time is still likely on our side. Just.

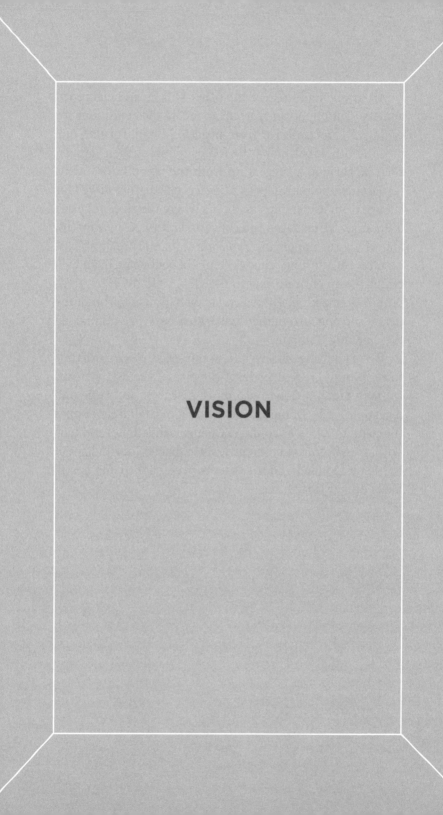

VISION

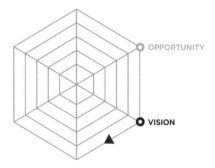

No one has *seen* the future. Not even those who describe themselves as 'futurists.' We will, however, through exploring the opportunity, have broadly imagined it as we'd like to see it. We'll want to share it as a common aspiration, a means of motivating others to help achieve it. In doing so, we try to reduce it to a sufficiently tangible and compelling proposition. The vision is, at the same time, the overarching reason for the change we're about to make happen, how we're going to get there and what it'll look like when we do. All in an impregnable conceptual and verbal nutshell. We then hope, having captured it, that we all see the same thing. On the face of it, that's unlikely.

The fundamental problem of vision statements is just this. However tight and grounded they may be, everyone pictures the destination differently. We further add our own frames of reference to the depiction, as we covered in Part One. With all of this we form a view as to whether we think the end is achievable and the means feasible, and whether the change is worthwhile.

THE VISION QUESTION

The problem and frustration may lie in the fact that the vision is so often generated as a *statement*. In doing so it allows us to challenge, refute or, worst of all, ignore it. However complex our mental mechanics, we can only process one big idea at a time. The more complex the idea, the more linear our thinking.

To counter this, some depict a series of punchy characteristics a vision must have. We do so with objectives we believe need to be SMART (specific, measurable, attainable, relevant and time-bound). We get rather hooked into these structures as we tend to love a checklist, especially one that's an acronym. Yet we find that DUMB works just as well for objectives – dynamic, understandable, motivating and believable. Who on earth would do that?

There's considerable evidence to support that asking a question increases the desired behaviour around the intent.[36] The more we contemplate a behaviour, the more likely we are to do it. A question, once asked, releases serotonin in our brain, and thereby takes over. While statements are inactive, questions are alive. We can't help but try to answer them. We're automatically engaged. It's called 'instinctive elaboration.' This is Daniel Kahneman's 'System 1' thinking, the fast, unconscious and emotional kit.[37] That is, as opposed to the more logical, rational and considered 'System 2.' Kahneman identified through experimentation that the two systems arrived at different conclusions by processing the same inputs. This has implications for the vision as for many colleagues it'll be their first interaction with the change initiative. We don't want it to be their last.

Questions can be just as aspirational and motivating as a proclamation. They also make us feel included and that we have an input to the response, rather than being simply told to imagine what was conceived in someone else's contemplation. We're involved. We can shape the outcome. The American writer and academic Amy Edmondson describes a leader at a children's hospital striving to achieve 100% patient safety by motivating with inquiry rather than instruction. She asked her team: "Tell me, what was your own experience this week, in the units, with your patients? Was everything as safe as you would like it to have been?"[38] With such a question, the power to motivate through gentle yet direct association is immense. It taps into our conscience. We have to be honest with, and answerable to, ourselves.

A question also helps with the potentially limiting nature of a statement. In being open-ended, it allows us to push on beyond the original aim if we find we have momentum or realize that we had set ourselves a target that transpired to be easy to attain. We're more likely to surprise ourselves.

Of course, they have the downside of implying that the asker has no answers. Otherwise, they wouldn't be asking a question, save as an introduction to how it'll be addressed. Leaders, after all, are supposed to have all the answers, or what are they for? I can safely imagine that you're now considering what leaders are for if they don't have answers. We can't help it.

STRUCTURING A VISION QUESTION

Visions need to satisfy several questions. So, we're using questions to form a question.

Why? It must be worthwhile doing this. There must be an opportunity to seize, that we have scoped. That may be an advantage to be gained, an innovation to harness or a competitive onslaught to repel. It must be something that makes us want to stop doing what we're doing and do this instead.

In the earliest instance we're asking a small group of people – our initiative and leadership team – to move from the default. They'll not bother if it's not worth it, or if it appears wasteful, unnecessary, misguided, sinister, vain, expensive, trivial or overblown.

How? We must be able to get there. It's pointless asking "How can we develop the technology that will get the first human on Saturn?" However beautiful and poetic a dream, it's just not going to happen in the poser's lifetime, if ever. Unlike our quest to reach the Moon – which once appeared fanciful but through commitment, passion, investment and a belief in its likely usefulness was realized – it's doubtful it's even worthwhile pursuing. However mysterious Saturn looks from afar, the evidence gathered to date tells us it's an ice-crusted gassed-out wasteland. An oft-quoted old Japanese proverb says that "Vision without action is a daydream; action without vision is a nightmare." It may just not be worthwhile acting in such an instance.

Equally, the question must ask how a transition may be achieved to a state sufficiently different from the present, without the temptation of loading the answer. We often already have a preloaded answer if we're close to the challenge.

An example may be:

> How can we become the world's
> household name for lawnmowers?

Instead of:
> To become the world's
> household name for lawnmowers.

If we opt for the latter, the statement, the very first question our colleagues will ask us is "How?" There will be an expectation that we have the answers and we're ready. We'll have instantly created a one-way 'impress me' situation, rather than a sense that we have something to aim for and we're to set about achieving it together.

What? We must be able to understand the place we're trying to get to, even if at this stage we only recognize it in terms of what we know today. In moving from horse-drawn carriage to automobile, as radical a change as that was, it was still focused on transporting groups of people quickly and safely from one place to the next within a secure(ish) container. The means of propulsion was the point of departure. There was enough of the core to convey the idea. Similarly, we didn't suddenly end up with a supercomputer in our pocket; the smartphone went through several steadily shrinking iterations before it got there.

Arching over all three questions is that a vision must be **understandable**. We need to avoid corporate jargon, acronyms, waffle, the stuff we (all, unfortunately, to some degree) mysteriously take on when we pass through the revolving door, however hard we try not to. We should say it as we'd speak it. Test it. We should run it by some people who aren't involved, whose feedback we trust. If those close to us don't get it, those who are vested certainly won't.

A vision question needs to be answered by everyone individually. For some, the response may be awkward, scary or simply not something that they can answer. For the rest, it's serotonin on tap – and they'll guide the others, too.

LIVING IN A
MESSAGE HOUSE

Looking a little like a kindergarten sketch, the message house is an incredibly useful and powerful way to consider, structure and develop a vision and its supporting objectives and proof points. I'm not sure who invented it, but thanks are deserved. Comprising a simple roof, joist and blockwork wall construction, it's all we need in graphical terms to organize our thinking. It's often used to get messaging straight after the fact or event. Its real strength for us though comes near the beginning of the initiative.

It looks something like Figure 16 in its structure:

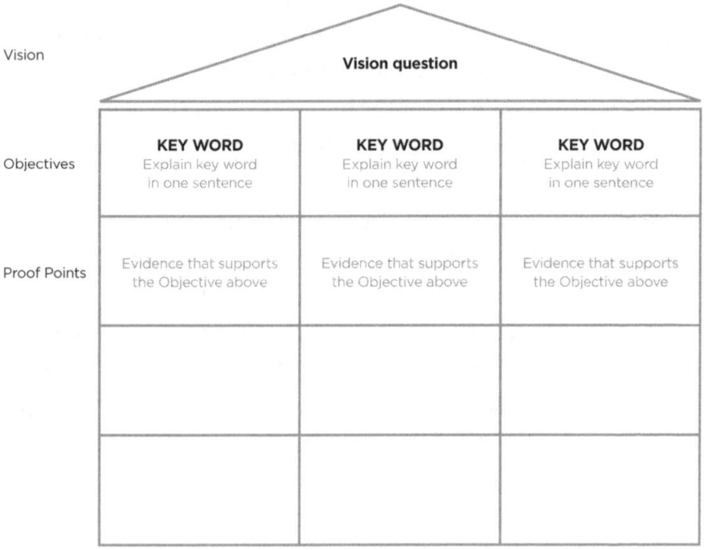

FIGURE 16

The vision question sits in the roof space. Everything hangs from it. The objectives act as the joists, breaking down the vision into tangible and measurable outcomes. Each is a longer, simple statement that serves to further explain the vision, grounded in recognizable reality. They should contain a quantitative element that makes it testable or measurable, or if not mentioned specifically then a path to such an element. The single-word roll-up for each objective makes each one memorable. It's recommended that the objectives are developed along with the vision. Together, these are the stable components of our initiative.

The vision and objectives are the things that get repeated. Everyone associated with the change initiative needs to know them and reinforce them. Over and over. They should stand up to scrutiny, using the supporting statements to strengthen the case. The crafting of the vision and objectives shouldn't be an exercise in corporate posturing or linguistic flamboyance. They should satisfy those criteria set out in 'Element 2: Message' in the chapter 'I'm informed.'

As an example, the vision and objectives for a necessary but unglamorous household consumer product may be something like Figure 17.

	AVAILABLE	AFFORDABLE	RELIABLE
Vision		How do we become the world's most desired and purchased [product] within two years?	
Objectives	Order from stock, supplied within 24 hours anywhere in the world – so no one has to wait	Innovation within everyone's reach at [price] RRP, the best value [product] of its kind – anywhere, ever	Tested beyond endurance, the [product] comes with a standard 3-year warranty
Proof Points	Evidence that supports the Objective above	Evidence that supports the Objective above	Evidence that supports the Objective above

FIGURE 17

Below each objective sit several 'proof points.' They're the substance, the blockwork walls of the house, the evidence where it exists and the detail where it doesn't (but may do, soon). Unlike the vision and objectives, the statements will evolve, some will drop away when no longer needed, to be replaced by others. While remaining a living document, there should always be enough substance to the walls to keep them supporting the vision and objectives. For instance, beneath the objective of 'reliable,' the proof point may be the ability of the new testing facility to process a given number of units per hour. That may start as an estimate and, as more is known, be tweaked to reflect the increased certainty.

It's important before finalizing the message house to revert to the opportunity map to ensure the two are aligned. Consideration of the vision and objectives may have taken us away from what originally inspired and galvanized us. It may have assumed a life of its own. One, or both, may need tweaking. We really do need to live inside our message house, with all the responsibilities associated with looking after a dwelling.

While the content is intended to see a great deal of the light of day, the message house is a construct that rarely appears in public in this form. That's not to say it shouldn't, of course. It's essentially a 'back room' tool, something for leadership and our core initiative team. It exists to frame and instil the key messages of the initiative, but they're then communicated in many ways at varying times, as we'll cover in Part Three.

We've now distilled our opportunity to a single question that will inspire, inform, galvanize and engage. We've clarified and explained it with three core objectives. We're ready to build the walls – the evidence.

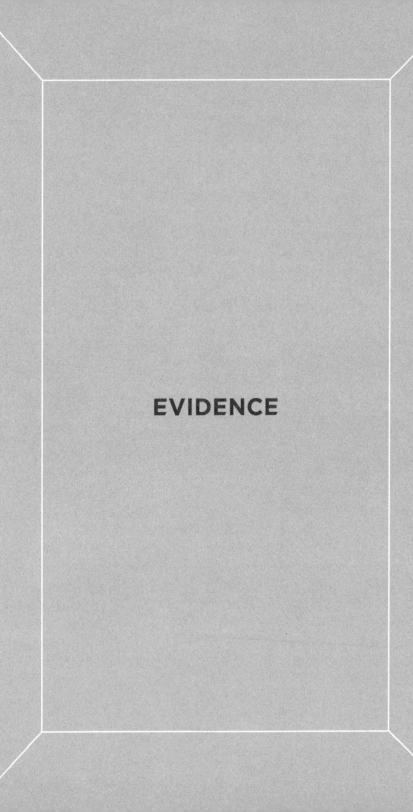

EVIDENCE

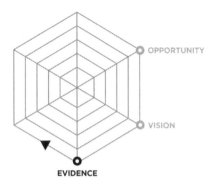

The walls of our message house – and therefore of our whole initiative – are comprised evidence. They need to stand up to a test of proof.

The Center for Evidence-Based Management (CEBMa), an independent not-for-profit group defines its primary practice interest as "making decisions through the conscientious, explicit and judicious use of the best available evidence from multiple sources."[39] This entails finding evidence, critically assessing it and applying it. It can be data, information, facts, research, precedent, experiences or stories. It may come from sources within the organization or external to it. We still apply our insight to evidence; it isn't an asset that has a life and purpose of its own.

In the manner in which we approach the opportunity, the evidence we gather supports where we've come from and how we got here, where we are now, and what we might do to get where we want. We strive to obtain as much as is useful and helpful, and we endeavour to be as prudent and sensible with it as possible.

The inherent trouble with evidence is that it's subject to almost unavoidable bias. Pure evidence and completely clean judgment are theoretical propositions achievable only under strict laboratory conditions. That which we are likely to gather rarely points to a clear conclusion as there's always a counter position using the same material. It's often gathered to support a pre-existing position in which case we sift out what may be useful and discard the rest. What's vital to remember is that none of the reasons that evidence may be impure are ever enough to have us believe it's *not* needed.

We first need to find it. It can come from a wide variety of sources. We then need to critically assess the evidence obtained, using *our* experience, resources, insight and intuition. Finally, we need to apply it to the decision-making process. Find, assess, apply.

Two aspects of evidence are worth exploring further, given their central role as actors in a change initiative – data and story. We've been using both to great effect since we lost our gills. Cave paintings tell us we used data to tell stories before we had language. They're just about the oldest change tools we have – an example recently discovered in Indonesia was created around 44,000 years ago.[40] As history tells us, evidence, data and story are most powerful when used seamlessly together. Stories are data with spirit.[41] They have emotion, which data grounds. Stories bring data to life, adding context, colour and meaning, making it accessible, interesting and relevant. We can rarely tell stories without data. Data lends impartial credibility to stories that make them real.

DATA

Our change initiative will be built on data in whichever form is appropriate. But data, nonetheless.

The 9th-century historian Nennius, author of *Historia Brittonum*, was a classic example of an accumulator of data, including facts, perspectives, anecdotes and artefacts. Commenting on his findings he said: "I heaped up all that I found."[42] There followed no analysis, no recommendations or actions, just data. Similarly, much of what we gather today remains in a 'Nennial' heap, as we struggle to effectively analyse what we've collected.

The sources of data may be internal or external to the organization. If we commission the capture of data relating to ourselves, we have the challenge of ensuring it's robust enough to stand scrutiny – sample sizes, methods and time periods. Its ours but may not be enough. If external, gathered via research (from case studies, papers or comparative studies), we have to prove sufficient relevance or similarity. It's enough but not ours.

Data will be of various types. Some of our data will be quantitative, some qualitative but these aren't the same as objective and subjective. Both quantitative and qualitative data can be either subjective or objective. Most of all, it has to be useful. It can be categorized against its usefulness as seen in Figure 18.

	Useless	Useful
Qualitative	Sometimes interesting or entertaining	Gives narrative framework to the quantitative data
Quantitative	Helpful in proving nothing is going on	Objective proof and determinant of solutions

DATA

Useless   Useful

USEFULNESS

FIGURE 18

What lies in each of the four panes has a contribution to make. We're not simply stating that the 'useless' panes are irrelevant. Credibility in most respects is often gossamer, yet especially so with data. We build this confidence over time. We may be interested in the useless data as it may give us a sense of completeness: we didn't see anything untoward or unusual, we had to check, and we've reduced our risk by doing so. We can gradually dispense with repeated useless data until we're convinced there's nothing else out there worth bothering with except for the core we've identified. It's therefore useful *because* it's useless. If the figures at the outer reaches are interesting or concerning, we'll bring them to the fore.

THE FOUR STAGES OF DATA

I've been fortunate to work with Artificial Intelligence (AI) genius Bruce Davison.[43] Much of this subsection is shaped by more insightful conversations with Bruce about data than I might have once imagined possible.

There are four stages to data as evidence: question, collection, analysis and action (Figure 19). After we have an idea, hunch or inkling, we formulate the question, gather data, analyse it and do what we deem appropriate or necessary (even if this is, after consideration, nothing at all). While some aspects of this book have questioned linearity, this is an area where, in most cases, sequence is helpful. Otherwise we're throwing things at the wall in the hope of something sticking. Anyone can do that, but few would recommend it.

First, the **question**. Data doesn't simply arrive with purpose. If data has no purpose, it's just noise. We must give it its purpose by asking the right questions. What are we trying to solve or change? It's not always as easy as it first appears. We then need to determine what data might be helpful in answering it. It necessitates that we ask good questions, or we'll get duff data: "garbage asked, garbage in" precedes "garbage in, garbage out." We can always get better at asking questions.

Second, **collection**. This should, in most instances, be a continual exercise. It's often amassed at the start of the initiative and used to formulate strategy and plan, but not kept up to date throughout. Much that's relevant may change between the collection point and completion, particularly as it's held that the change occurring around us is accelerating.[44] One-time data collection may lead to spurious conclusions unless our question relates merely to a point in time.

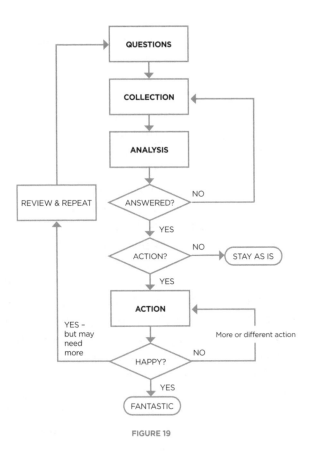

FIGURE 19

Our data will often be vulnerable. Its quality and robustness are rarely uniform. A small gap, error or inconsistency in the data set presents a glaring opportunity for sceptics to shred the whole lot, even if the rest is sound. I once worked for a razor-sharp company director whom I could guarantee would always find the one bit of data in my business case that was more assumption than evidence. I could see his eyes flicker across my spreadsheet and be drawn to it like a moth to a flame. After several embarrassing pitches I flipped the process and admitted straight out of the blocks where my data was weak and why, how I had arrived at it and what flexibility we had if my assumptions were incorrect by any degree. It strengthened my case on each occasion thereafter.

Third, **analysis**. After the accumulation we need to hunt through the heap of data to see if anything makes sense. We seek patterns or trends that may help with explaining the past or present, and thereby offering clues to the future. This may either be specifically related to the data set itself, or from its general nature and flavour. We organize and structure what we've gathered. We bring our insight and contextual knowledge to bear. Sometimes, however robust our process and however hard we look, there may be no discernible patterns, in which case our judgment becomes essential. While technology can help, and at the time of writing is getting better at doing so, it's still a very human discipline in many fields. The challenge of identifying and eradicating bias will remain, however more effectively automated analysis becomes.

Finally, we have to consider what **action** the analysed data will prompt in answer to the original question. This might be a human activity, or it can be run through an application or system. AI will increasingly be developed and applied in this fourth stage of data. The human will still be very much in the loop, recognizing nuances, applying insight and judgment in making decisions. However, in many instances we won't need to undertake the time-consuming grunt work. Nor will we need to try to simultaneously solve multiple problems in an unhelpfully linear fashion, as we're programmed to do. The robots will do the robotic stuff, so we no longer have to.

While our data collection may be continuous, we shouldn't operate under the assumption that a single pass of the four stages will be sufficient. It's rarely enough that it ends at action. We often find we need to **review and repeat**, possibly adjusting each stage from the question through to the decision on what to do. It's not deemed to be a stage of data in its own right but is certainly a likely activity. In a world where nothing stands still, neither should our data.

There's a trust issue with data, too. We have to trust it in itself, as data, appropriately collected, responding to the right questions. If, indeed, we trust the questions we've asked.

We have to trust ourselves or those from whom we request help to analyse it skillfully and meaningfully. We have to trust the analysis, or the technology deployed to prompt the right action. And we have to trust that we're doing the right thing (and doing it right) as a result of the preceding stages. Across the four stages of data that's a lot of trust interfaces, which means a host of points at which our evidence could be doubted – by others or perhaps even ourselves. So, we can't scrimp or short-circuit the data process, or we'll struggle to look in the mirror.

BIG DATA

A word on Big Data, the great hope of the 2010s and touted as likely to become the world's most valuable resource. It would, it was commonly asserted, solve everything, even science itself. Yet quantity doesn't guarantee quality. As we've found in our own personal lives, the exponential increase in the amount of data available to us requires vastly improved search, filtration and understanding capabilities. Behold, too, the proportionate loss of trust in its viability.

The increasingly opaque use of data for achieving political ends has similarly eroded trust in its gathering and use. It's placed a further demand on our filtration process to include the need to routinely check sources and facts. The use of data for 'gaslighting' – leading us to question our own perception, judgment and even sanity – has regrettably become common practice in recent years.

We often rush to gather as much data as possible on a given situation and run the four-stage process on it all. However, an understanding of dependencies might see us do this differently.

If x and y are subject to a single round of data collection, we may conclude that they behave similarly and act on them as such, never discovering a dependency. Even if we suspect that y is dependent on x, if we gather all the data in one go, our analysis may well point to a different action than if we first analyse x and take the required action, then subsequently evaluate y. Patience, if time and budget allow, can gift insight and prevent a lot more time and money being spent on re-working the entire exercise.

Finally, we need to beware of the assumption that data is universally welcome. Data can be revealing. That's rather the hope when we pose the questions it's intended to answer. Yet such revelations may create awkwardness or embarrassment. It may show that the strategy pursued to date was in error or poorly executed. It may reveal waste or inefficiency on our watch. Data can therefore in some situations be somewhat dangerous. For this reason, its collection and analysis may be declined. When we surface insight from data for our change initiative, we have to keep it pointing forward. It shouldn't ever be used for scoring points.

STORY

Stories are data, just different data. They weave the quantifiable and verifiable with the personal, experiential and embellished. They can have a power that data alone can only dream of. They're as old as humanity itself. Plato went as far as to say, "Those who tell the stories rule society."[45] Recently it's become vogue to call stories 'narrative' because it sounds more business-like, but it's the same thing.

The *Epic of Gilgamesh*, a poem from Mesopotamia written in Akkadian and only discovered in 1853, is generally regarded as the oldest written story, dating back to around 1800 BCE. Yet for much of our history, storytelling was oral, conducted with the aid of drawings, gestures and symbols, passed through countless generations. Aesop's 725 moral fables created in the 500s BCE weren't actually written down until around 300 years later. In many societies this persisted until comparatively recently. Native American tribes didn't begin to record their stories until after contact with European settlers.

Stories have the capacity to captivate, to hold our attention and fire our imagination. They enable intrigue, suspense, twists and surprises. Hindsight allows us to aggrandize and weave threads through stories, to bring their relevance up to date. In a quote attributed to the golfer Lee Trevino, "The older I get the better I used to be."[46] They also allow us to paint pictures of the future we want or hope to see – or in some cases, don't.

For leaders and rebels alike, stories create connection, empathy and alignment. They can express the vulnerability and fragility of humanity. They can also simplify complex ideas and difficult challenges. They encapsulate the values we looked at in Part One, especially when told in parable form. We're habituated to stories too, as there's a restricted palette of structures, and we generally fit what we're told into one of those models. Part of the work is already done for us.

Stories are everywhere in an organization. Much of the time we don't look for them or aren't conscious that what we're hearing is a story. We can make a 'Nennial' heap of them too – they're not all useful. The challenge is finding those that are. We can usually feel them, through the degree to which they *resonate*. We can sense ourselves in them.

Leaders need stories, in both directions – to hear and gather them as evidence and to tell them. The latter may belong in some senses in Part Three of the book, but we're going to cover it here. To a huge extent story weaves its way through the whole of this book, as it should.

HEARING STORIES

As leaders of change, we need to **hear** stories. They're cultural vessels. Not the sort of culture mapped out on a whiteboard on an executive awayday, but what's *really* happening. Collecting and collating stories is vital leadership behaviour, especially at a time of uncertainty. Taking the time to listen is therefore vital. In organizational life, the strength of feeling is, for most, far better conveyed when spoken than written. When we read stories, we often do so in a voice that seems appropriate. They're also far more likely to contain unrestrained emotion than a crafted note. There's less potential for judgment of, and consequence for, the teller.

As with data, the sources of stories may be internal or external to the organization. If we seek to surface and capture stories relating to ourselves, we have the challenge of ensuring our methods and time periods are robust. Achieving this is very often more difficult than collecting quantifiable data. As with data too, if external, gathered via research, we have to prove sufficient relevance or similarity to our challenge. External stories are often better when related to more universal or principled points.

TELLING STORIES

As leaders of change, we need to **tell** stories. Just as with data, the selection of useful stories must be rigorous, and their relevance and meaning beneficial. Much as case-making methods more commonly associated with organizational life are necessary, there's no passion in a bullet point. We'd usually rather hear a colleague's story than their business strategy, even though at times we need to listen to the latter. For those of us listening, we don't feel as though we're being lectured to, the slides, charts and stats aren't grinding us into the dust. If we can have the story contain our business strategy, the evidence needed and how we're going to get there, we're in business. It lives, and it'll be remembered.

Yet despite our exposure to literature, film, theatre and our memories of bedtime tales over our formative years, we often still need guidance in storytelling. Here is a quick guide. I'm indebted to the work of Shawn Callahan in Australia for my exposure to the power of storytelling in organizations, and so for a more in-depth study of the subject his book *Putting Stories to Work: Mastering Business Storytelling*[47] is well worth sourcing. There's probably some of Shawn's inspiration in here.

We need to do the following, in no particular order:
- **Free flow into it**: we shouldn't say "I'm going to tell you a story." Those unprepared to listen will switch off. It's like

when I used to say, "I'm going to read you a poem." Although perhaps for many people that was worse ...

- **Know it**: this may sound daft, but we shouldn't tell a story we can't quite remember. We'll lose the audience's attention.
- **Have a structure we're comfortable with**: this will help with pacing and recall. Stories should neatly break into bite-sized chunks.
- **Be relevant**: we should make sure it has some cultural, organizational or situational grounding appropriate to who we're talking to, where we are and the matter we're addressing.
- **Maintain pace**: we should create a rhythm we feel at ease talking at. Play a drumbeat to our self if it helps. We should always watch for the energy of our listeners and be ready to change pace if we see or sense it dropping.
- **Create suspense**: we should create and maintain the sense that something significant is about to happen.
- **Test our humour**: if we think we're going to be funny, we should make sure we know it's funny. The silence and tumbleweed at the end of what we believe to be a cracking gag is crushing. It's embarrassing for the listener, too.
- **Use the pause**: it's incredibly powerful when we want to create suspense or surprise or want to underline that what we just said is important. We can also potentially repeat the gist of the key point if we think it got lost in the flow.
- **Ensure we don't digress too far**: one stage is fine, but two stages are risky. We may not find our way back and we'll be lost telling a different story from the one we started, with a different point entirely. We should always return quickly.
- **Pivot the story on the unexpected**: there must be something that lands with a thud, that makes the listener take notice.

If we think "I'm just rubbish at telling stories," we probably don't realize just quite how much we tell or use them. They may not be quite as short as Ernest Hemingway's 'six word' stories, but they may be close. We should unravel our day.

Find the stories we told. Then retell them with reference to the foregoing.

However many channels exist today for the sharing of stories, as human beings we still carry them with us, in the manner of the earliest traditions. Stories will change as people arrive and leave, and we, our organization and our colleagues change. As with data, gathering and telling stories shouldn't be a static process. While some stories have a power and resonance that render them timeless, many are 'of the moment.' Wider social norms and attitudes, and with them our world view, change too. Our rejection today of what we struggle to think was once acceptable has been evident at the time of writing. Statues of those whose acts and attitudes – once celebrated in bronze – are now regarded by modern standards as anything from repugnant to barbaric, are being torn down. The associated stories, once told with pride, become warnings from history. At our scale, new stories will emerge from events and ideas during the course of our initiative. Similarly, as leaders we'll need to tell stories from the immediate present that will help shape the future.

A word of caution, however: powerful as they are, we shouldn't overdo stories. They're most effective when used sparingly, at the right time. Usually when a point needs landing, or a difficulty needs overcoming. Using *too many stories* is just as inadvisable as too few. We must ensure they have enough 'white space' to make an impact.

We'll go one stage deeper for a moment with a core component of stories that can be extracted and used as shorthand for conveying the core of the meaning – *metaphor*. 'Core' of the meaning. As if to 'illustrate,' we're using them all the time.

METAPHORS

Metaphors are as vital and ubiquitous in storytelling as they are in general conversation. They help us explain something in terms of something else. This is achieved by either simplifying to make the meaning clearer or more relatable, or by enriching or mystifying to add magic to the mundane.

Metaphors are usually based around symbols (which we'll cover in Part Three), each of which has a degree of shared meaning (we all understand it similarly) and a meaning personal to just us. If we said our change programme was as "balanced as a ballerina," we'd be fairly aligned as we conjured the ballerina, the symbol in the metaphor. Yet no two people would have exactly the same picture in mind. We may recall different performances, as well as different sensory experiences and associated memories of it such as how it made us feel at the time. This all contributes to our personal understanding of the metaphor, and so we give it our own particular gist, even if the meaning is roughly the same for everyone.

Metaphors can create a lasting impact, having a benchmark effect. I recall a beer advert from many years ago where after the usual passage of the promotion, it ended with, "Like an angel cryin' on your tongue."[48] You can tell me all about purity laws and organic hops and prehistoric recipes, but I've never forgotten the metaphor. Even though the brand in question wasn't to my taste, all other beers since have, to me, been compared in similar terms.

The emotion associated with change will often cloud our reason. Effective metaphors woven into stories are probably the most important means of creating meaning and association where it appears difficult to land. Of course, they can also be useful when the same approach is used in conveying a response to a proposed change. The trading of metaphors may just be the common language that creates the connection needed.

Too many in succession, or their use when not needed, can feel awkward at the receiving end. As with stories themselves, powerful and timeless as they can be their use, particularly the overt, needs to be restrained, deployed only when the effect is needed.

Or we could just use smiley faces. More on that in Part Three ☺.

LEADERSHIP

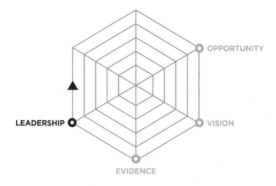

For all but the most ardent of self-organizing communitarians operating in exceptional times,[49] change needs leadership. 'Delivering change' could be considered to be item one on any leadership role description, irrespective of where and with whom. We're assuming it's what we've been asked to do.

As a change leader, we connect the points of the spider chart of our operating system as the pursuer of the opportunity, the custodian of the vision, the gatherer of evidence, the creator and protector of trust, and the securer of the resources. That said, while as leader we can potentially do a huge amount of good (and harm, of course), the absence of, or damage to, any component of the operating system can undermine it.

We looked at leadership from a conceptual standpoint in Part One. We now need to consider the type of leadership we'll bring. So, this chapter is all about us.

LEADER TYPES

After three and a half decades in a variety of sectors and countries, I've observed that there are two broad strands of leadership: technical and spirited. We rarely encounter those who are outstandingly good at both. Of course, we often find leaders who aren't especially good at either. Both types satisfy our earlier characterization of leaders as opposed to managers. Bear in mind leaders are often caricatured, but we'll probably recall someone who fits each just as we'll recall those who don't. It's always worthwhile knowing which we are and having that validated. It's been known for a long time that self-awareness is a gift that keeps on giving. "Know thyself" was one of the 147 maxims inscribed on the Temple of Delphi in the 4th century BCE.

First, there are **technical** leaders, who always respond exactly to the letter. They often bring order, reason, calm, numeracy, IQ and authority, commanding respect without too much emotion. They make sure there's no chance of anyone going off the cliff, because they know they'll need them later. Think metaphorical (and sometimes real) black and yellow tape. They tend to come from (but not exclusively) professions that value accuracy over speed, such as Finance, Legal and HR.

Then, there are **spirited** leaders who bring empathy, connection, equity, inspiration, EQ (emotional intelligence), humour, insight, courage, judgment and power. In getting stuff done they're liable to leave a trail of chaos of varying degrees behind them. They exhibit confidence over and above a grasp of reality as, in many respects, reality is a restrictive inconvenience. They inspire and are admired, yet their flaws often make them easier to respect for what they do and how they make us feel, than for who they are. They're happy for us to follow them off a cliff because they're convinced it'll be worthwhile and they don't imagine it'll hurt. They tend to come from professions that value speed over accuracy, such as marketing, design or innovation.

Naturally, these are generalizations, and they make no reference to global or local context, pressure or priorities. It's quite possible for leaders to transition from the spirited to the technical or vice versa, sparked by a perspective-changing event or experience. Nothing is fixed.

The reality is that in almost all instances, threads from both types are needed in leading change. Inspiration and vision are at their most potent when combined with evidence and acumen. Knowing when to act is best matched with an understanding of when to be patient. EQ and IQ are at their most compelling when operating in tandem.

The two types are often manifested in different people. If we're too much of one, we'll need to find the other and bring them close, ensuring we both recognize what we each bring. There's nothing wrong at all with that. As mentioned, being both types of leader in equal measure and fine balance is quite rare.

ORGANIZATIONAL CONSIDERATIONS

Yet it's not quite as straightforward as all this. There are three key organizational influences on our leadership approach.

First, the **network**. It's far easier when planning for us to think of organizations as straightforward and predictable command-and-control structures, with clean and unimpeded lines of communication and all the certainty that brings. In such a case, leading change would be a matter of issuing clear instructions and enjoying the expected response (by which I mean the instruction being carried out, not two fingers). Invariably they're not. While not everyone will be in the midst of experimenting with new organizational approaches like direct democracy, loosely structured holacracy[50] or the free form of Ricardo Semler,[51] there will be infinite variations on the standard-issue military-based model. It's usual, too, that commands are rarely specific, often need interpretation, are subject to the judgment of the recipient and only partially followed. While command-and-control has generated significant prosperity over the last few centuries, think 'Charge of the Light Brigade' during the Crimean War for just about everything that *can* go wrong with such an approach.

The *real* organization chart – not the published version, which is the first of two maps – is a complex web of relationships and influence. This is our second map, the organizational network. We'll need to decouple, bend and shape the way the organization represents itself as a pyramid to reflect the reality as we see it. It's damned difficult to draw. Every organization will be entirely unique and will change over time, often frequently. So, just when we think we've nailed it, we'll have to keep redrawing. We'll meet hard and soft connections, authority and influence, travelling in all directions. We'll need to think about where we are in relation to what we need to achieve. In particular, we'll need to consider the breaks in connectivity. They're crevices. Good intentions, ideas or information can be lost within them forever. Chances are we won't be where we need to be, and we'll need to consider in our planning how we migrate.

The 'coalitionists' lose some traction here. Management theorists tend to think, naturally, in terms of management, and so tend to envisage coalitions as being team or function heads, or aspiring executives who, brimming with confidence, bring their own seats with them in case they need a table. It's not a case of gathering a collection of those imbued with ambition and authority. It's about understanding where the real power and influence lies, as it shifts, and harnessing it. The coalitions themselves will alter in composition and purpose over the course of the initiative. As leaders we must try to read it in practice.

Second, **accountability**. We're never alone. As leaders we're still likely to be answerable to others, so it doesn't all rest with us. We'll have peers, with whom we'll need to align and stay aligned. We'll bring in colleagues and delegate, so we'll maintain shared accountability. In a similar vein to understanding the shifting forces at play, mapping accountability and delegated authority in multiple directions isn't as easy as drawing an organigram with a few arrows pointing people at other people. Accountability doesn't always translate into formal authority structures, particularly where technical or specialist skills are involved. It often varies by circumstance, for example, proximity to the customer.

A word of caution, however. Consciously and deliberately spreading accountability, like buttering toast, to arrive at a 'can't fire us all' situation can lead to paralysis. This type of avoidance isn't a solution. Neither should it be confused with democratization. We just need to understand, as we're pacing the house at 4 am wondering if we're ever going to make it work, that we're not shouldering the entire responsibility. We must avoid the temptation to email our colleagues at this time in the hope they're wide awake with worry, too.

Which brings us onto the third aspect, **uniqueness**. As we covered in Part One, each organization is a jumble of personalities, preferences, habits and traits that we won't find exactly replicated anywhere else. It means that absolutely every change initiative is a one-off. People arrive and leave. What worked in one organization may not work in another. What worked once in one place may not work in the same place again. It's the confounded river and those about to step in it. Learning and experience must be complemented by open-mindedness and context-appreciative frames of reference. We're likely to be a relatively well-informed rookie with every initiative we lead, and it's dangerous to think any other way.

In many respects as leaders we might also strive to be what I once saw termed a 'serial incompetent'[52] whereby we pursue a role until we've mastered it, then choose something new and begin again. We become familiar with the sensation of starting afresh and we're happy to acknowledge it. Aside from some simple sense, life experience and a willingness to learn, we're aware we're entirely green. We appreciate in this state that we need to draw on the wisdom, expertise and skills of others, and our primary modus operandi is inquiry. As former US president Calvin Coolidge is reputed to have said: "No man ever listened himself out of a job."[53]

Whether we're considering organizational or specific change initiative leadership, or whether we're a technical or spirited leader (or both), the same style-agnostic principles apply.

They often make uncomfortable reading as we have to face up to a number of personal truths. We could probably write an essay on each pairing (many others have) that I've set out in Table 7. They've been listed in the alphabetical order of the 'Do This ...' column.

DO THIS ...	... NOT THIS
Admit when wrong	Assign blame
Admit when don't know	Bluster
Ask questions	Give opinions
Be available	Be busy
Be accountable to your team	Be accountable to yourself
Be optimistic – it can be done	Be pessimistic – it can't be done
Be present	Hide
Be specific	Be vague
Delegate	Take it on – be a martyr
Discover	Assume
Do as you'd like others to do	Do as you like
Empathize	Antagonize
Encourage difference	Enforce homogeneity
Family first	Self first
Follow up	Ignore
Get out of the way	Block
Give credit	Take credit

Give regular feedback	Stay silent
Guide behaviour	Create rules
Include	Exclude, select
Invite expertise	Promote the amateur
Laugh at yourself	Laugh at others
Learn	Lecture
Listen	Talk
Match words and behaviours	Say one thing, do another
Macromanage	Micromanage
Open up	Close down
Prioritize your people	Prioritize your boss
Protect	Expose
Provide clarity	Obfuscate
Reflect	Deflect
Respect	Inspect
Share	Withhold
Show vulnerability	Admit no weakness
Simplify	Complicate
Take responsibility	Cover your arse
Trust	Suspect
Unite and solve	Divide and rule
Welcome the possibility	Fear the risk

TABLE 7

We can use this table to create a leadership behaviour map. It requires us to be honest with ourselves and others – and have them be honest with us. I doubt anyone could claim not to venture into the '... Not This' column at any time. Such a claim in itself would be a step inside the line. Even, that is, under the most pressing of circumstances or on the most ferociously burning platform. Our behaviour shouldn't deteriorate in proportion to the difficulty of the challenge. We can still be exceptional leaders in times of great pressure.

We can identify where we need to improve, and what strategies we can put in place to do so. We would need to gather evidence in support of the present and to help target the future we want to see, so it's fortunate we covered it in the previous chapter. No excuses here.

We may even need to get some help from specialists and be open about that too, because next we're covering trust.

To be effective for our initiative, it would need everyone on, or associated with, the leadership team to do so. That said, while we're in the throes of persuasion there's nothing wrong with a little self-improvement. What we can guarantee is, whether conscious or not, the difference will be noticeable. It's not an approach born out of theory, just decent human behaviour that can allow others to be the best they can be.

We may be seeking even greater brevity than the above summary of a warehouse stuffed with leadership literature in our attention-starved world. An excellent list of what makes an effective and human-centric leader by the illustrator of my previous book, Simon Heath, is taken from his blog *Murmuration*.[54] Simon reduces what's needed to just 25 words (Figure 20). We could even say he has been slightly extravagant here, and trim a few. Like – "Do the right thing, do things right and don't be an arse." Or perhaps just "Don't be an arse" covers it by implication. Being an arse is no qualification for successfully leading change. It can be that simple if we want it to be. Often, we find that what we begin with is enough.

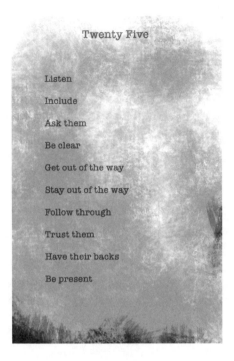

Twenty Five

Listen

Include

Ask them

Be clear

Get out of the way

Stay out of the way

Follow through

Trust them

Have their backs

Be present

FIGURE 20

A final thought. Leadership has an occasional tendency to become ego-driven, in which the personality *becomes* the vision. It's very rarely a conscious decision resulting from philosophical pondering.[55] This may be an inherent trait of the individual or it can accumulate from the intense stress of the situation, where elevated isolation appears to the leader to be the only escape route from the enveloping chaos. In such instances, the leader becomes the sole architect, arbiter and driver of change, the singular 'top' in 'top-down.' It harks to the perception of the 'gold standard' of change we mentioned in the Opening Gambit. The signs are often clear at an early stage, even if there aren't yet determined-looking portraits plastered over the sides of buildings. History tells us this never ends well, even in a localized organizational setting.

TRUST

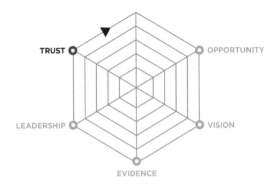

Trust is everywhere. As the firm belief in the reliability of someone or something, it underpins the functioning of human society. We experience it unconsciously every day. Norms of behaviour determine that there are things we do instinctively and naturally, and things we don't do. Philosophers have differed over whether this is driven by fear or care, when in reality it's both, but the outcome is the same: humanity functions on trust. It does it very well, too.

Yet if we were to read the related internet blogs and the pages of management journals, we might be forgiven for thinking that trust is in short supply in the corporate world. We could conclude that we spend our time seeking out the weaknesses and vulnerabilities in others in pursuit of personal gain, irrespective of the harm we may cause.

The problem is that in a corporate setting where, as strangers, we're brought together in the hope that we'll like (and like working with) one another, our radar is tuned. When the pressure of change is added, ever-smaller breaches or lapses of trust can be magnified and have significant and lasting consequences. Our radar at this time is therefore hyper tuned. Relationships, processes and systems held together by shared values and purpose and regarded as stable begin to lose their veneer of comfortable predictability when we're not sure how they'll settle. We're constantly looking for both proof of trust's survival and signs of it having broken down. We're considering where we might place our stock of trust. We believe it (incorrectly) to be finite.

As leaders of change we're called on to build, nurture and develop trust in what we're trying to achieve, the people around us and within our team, and everyone affected by the change. Trust faces in all directions. A tough job just got a whole lot tougher. We're doing it in front of a live studio audience, too.

We need to look at it in two ways: one we shall simply call 'trust' as this relates to our individual relationships; the other that has become known as 'psychological safety' as it operates at a group level.

INDIVIDUAL TRUST

There's still an outstanding question as to whether we're essentially trusting creatures.

Philosophers in previous centuries would tend to trace humanity back to a time before records began to try to establish human character in an innocent 'state of nature.' For Thomas Hobbes it was a scary place. He described in *Leviathan* (1651) our life in this age as "solitary, poor, nasty, brutish, and short"[56] – which reminds me of some people I've worked with over the years (often without the 'poor'). Others like Jean-Jacques Rousseau concluded that we once enjoyed universal and unquestioned trust until someone ruined it all. He declared in a 1754 essay: "The first person who, having enclosed a plot of land, took it into his head to say this is mine and found people simple enough to believe him was the true founder of civil society ... You are lost if you forget that the fruits of the earth belong to all and the earth to no one!"[57] It implies that we've been battling with trust ever since. Philosophy doesn't offer us any conclusion as in this regard it's all conjecture. But whatever route we took, we managed to get through it and are here today.

In organizational terms trust can deliver significant benefits. It can help people work more effectively together, solve problems more easily, encourage openness and honesty, relieve us of overbearing rules and structures, help develop common values, promote predictability and certainty, and make us and our teams more effective performers.[58] It can, in short, make change easier and more successful.

Trust is a personal thing. We have it, show it, give it and receive it. It's a great liberator. We think and act so much more freely when unencumbered by a concern that others may act prejudicially. We refer to this as operating within a *condition* of trust. It's incredibly easy for us to gift, we just have to do so. Ernest Hemingway, in a private letter, once wrote: "The way to make people trustworthy is to trust them."[59]

While it's an individual thing, we all have a part to play in maintaining the collective condition. It's everyone's responsibility. Yet it's fragile and delicate. Like a stack of Jenga blocks, it takes a long time to build and a very short time to collapse, often with one misguided action. We're often likely to do or say something that gives rise to our colleagues thinking perhaps trust has broken down, when we simply haven't thought through the consequences of what we've said or done (or not). If the condition – or atmosphere – of trust is right, then accidental transgressions can be easily forgiven and absorbed. So, while trust is an individual thing, when lots of people co-exist there's a gestalt element in that the sum of the parts is other than the whole. We forget sometimes that it starts with ourselves. The more we trust ourself, the more we're disposed toward trusting others.

Trust breaks down when motives start to be questioned, and we begin to think "But *what if* ...?" We may well witness those *pretending* to trust, showing what has become termed 'cordial hypocrisy.'[60] The appearance of trust can be relatively easily mastered to cloak the pursuit of a personal agenda. Any suspicion of such within a team only serves to undermine trust for everyone. We'll all be what-iffing.

Trust exists in an organization on a scale from complete to absent, with a spectrum of caution between. It's rarely absolute. Yet we constantly introduce features that advertise that we doubt trust can exist. Contracts, Human Resources (HR) systems, tracking applications that Frederick Winslow Taylor[61] would have been proud of under the broad banner 'people analytics,' are all clear in that rules and confidence in them are necessary, fundamental. Far more Hobbes than Rousseau, as we explored earlier.

As leaders in this environment we have an added dimension. We set the tone and the benchmark. We can create, build, repair and, if we're not careful, destroy trust. And as we need our colleagues to take on board what we say and do to deliver the change required, it's critical. We can eradicate the suspicion and doubt that serves to undermine trust. We can be the leaders we described in the previous chapter. No one ever thinks of a mistrustful environment as motivating, fun or productive. In fact, quite the opposite.

There are both personal and situational factors in the position we take on the matter, as offered by Robert Hurley in his 'trust model.'[62] This gives rise to strategies available to ensure trust is prevalent at all times, that the needle is slid to the right. I've abridged Hurley's model from the initial ten factors to the seven shown in Figure 21.

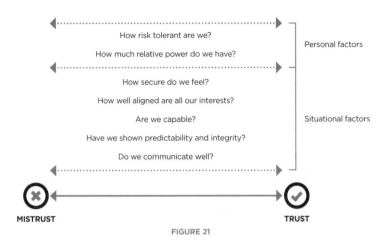

How risk tolerant are we?

How much relative power do we have?

Personal factors

How secure do we feel?

How well aligned are all our interests?

Are we capable?

Have we shown predictability and integrity?

Do we communicate well?

Situational factors

MISTRUST

TRUST

FIGURE 21

As a leadership team we can identify where we stand in relation to each and develop strategies to promote trust and mitigate mistrust. We can apply examples of attitudes and behaviours that signify we are beneficially changing the environment. It's even better if we develop those strategies with the participation of our team, acting as we mean to continue. As Hemingway suggested, nothing works better for building trust than trusting – and openly demonstrating it.

FROM PSYCHOLOGICAL TO ELEMENTAL SAFETY

When Google tried to understand what makes a great team, an initiative begun in 2012 that they grandly called Project Aristotle[63] (our Ancient Greeks, again), they spent a year crunching all the data they could find looking for patterns in more than a hundred teams. They drew a blank with their initial approach. Yet through many of the stories they gathered they began to align observations of teams characterized by high levels of trust and respect with academic papers focussed on the idea of 'psychological safety.' They had stumbled on the answer rather by accident.

The slightly clunky term (and I can say that here, of course, without a concern at being judged) was originally coined by William Kahn in 1990 in a journal paper. As he described it, possibly as awkwardly as the term itself: "Psychological safety was experienced as feeling able to show and employ one's self without fear of negative consequences of self-image, status or career. People felt safe in situations in which they trusted that they would not suffer for their personal engagement."[64]

Unlike trust per se, it necessarily exists at a group level. Trust is a key ingredient of psychological safety. It's a space for – as a later champion of the idea, Amy Edmondson, describes it – 'safe conflict.'[65] That is, a space where we can take risks, speak our minds, experiment, critique, raise concerns, show vulnerability and respect differences without fear of judgment or reproach. It's not a 'safe place,' where contrary views are buried, and no one confronts anything difficult or revealing. It's where we can speak up.

A lack of psychological safety in a team can be serious, all the way to terminal. Very often the reasons it doesn't exist are organizational. The founder of Corporate Rebels, Joost Minnaar, quotes three real-life corporate disasters of recent years which he considers had the same underlying psychological safety problem created by "hierarchically and bureaucratically run organizations operating with command-and-control, trying to motivate by fear and intimidation."[66] The environments were both untrusting at an individual level and psychologically unsafe at a group level.

It's an incredibly powerful idea. Yet it may be developed further in two respects. First, those running Project Aristotle realized that it was the way people *felt* that determined whether a team was successful. Those within were able to openly express emotion and vulnerability. William Kahn even described it as such, in his quote, three paragraphs back. As we often entwine how we instinctively feel with the measured positions we take, it may make sense to divide psychological safety into:

- **Rational safety**: where we are confident, we can form a view or argument and take a stance on an issue – whether we choose to express it or not – without concern at being judged or penalized for what we think or say; and
- **Emotional safety**: where we are fearless in expressing ourselves in any variety of ways. Not just in conversation – words may never even be spoken in doing so. It doesn't mean we don't expect a reaction, just that we don't feel that it will be in any way damaging.

Second, we can include physical safety. The landscape may not be as dangerous today as it might have been during the Middle Ages and in some instances of social upheaval, beyond, where speaking out of turn, or even just being accused or suspected of doing so, could arbitrarily result in our head in a basket – but it's a serious consideration, nonetheless.

There are three reasons for it being so. First, the manifestation of physical threat in the form of intimidation. Women the world over have experienced this even as their presence and influence in the workplace have grown, sometimes becoming an actual physical encroachment or attack. The prevalence of sexual harassment and abuse drove the rise from 2017 of the #MeToo movement, to publicly hold those responsible to account. Indeed, intimidation has been felt by many who have found themselves in a minority in any given situation, either for the way they are or the way they choose to be.

Second, the Covid-19 pandemic that began in 2019. The everyday use of the term 'personal protective equipment' (PPE) during the crisis has elevated our awareness of the critical importance of physical safety. 'Social distancing' – remaining a given physical distance from one another to avoid the transmission of the virus – is expected at the time of writing to be a requirement until the disease can be controlled or vaccinated against. The anxiety created by the risk of becoming infected as a result of partaking in what were once everyday activities will likely outlast any practical measures. As, too, will the post-traumatic stress suffered by many of those providing front-line health care and other essential services while the majority of the population have been required to remain at home.

Finally, as a further consideration in regard to physical safety, in more isolated communities there is often only one major employer. In such locations, organizational change that seems logical and sensible at a distant HQ may have a negative material impact on the community. I've worked on a number of such initiatives where an awareness of personal risk as the carrier of the corporate message can be unnerving.

As the term therefore fully encompasses how we think, feel and act we might, instead, call it 'elemental safety.' It appears as shown in Figure 22, and reflects the structure of Part Three of the book:

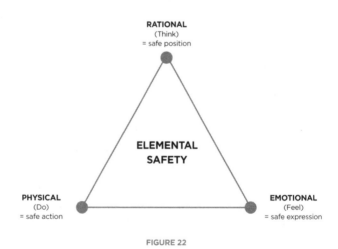

FIGURE 22

In the situations we face, one of the three aspects is likely to be dominant and all three may not be present simultaneously, but the model allows us to gather a complete picture of group-level trust.

It may, however, not all be a rush to safety. There are some cautious voices. Mark de Rond argues that it's beneficial only up to a point and that thereafter can mitigate against creativity where teams place "a higher premium on harmony than on solving the problem in hand."[67] The world of sport is littered with examples of teammates who trusted each other in the arena, where they had to, yet hated each other off it. Teddy Sheringham and Andy Cole at Manchester United played together marvellously in the 1990s but detested each other off the pitch. "I would rather sit down and have a cuppa with Neil Ruddock, who broke my leg in two places in 1996, than with Teddy Sheringham," Cole said.[68]

Yet these thoughts are outliers, simply to be aware of. I've worked in teams in the past where, despite the outward perception of harmony and the achievement of success against recognizable criteria, they were rationally and emotionally unsafe. Yet in these instances it wasn't an accident of personality or circumstance, or an immaturity, but an engineered strategy to keep everyone guessing, watching over their shoulder, striving to prove themselves daily. The strategy was considered to be a driver of performance. Bearing the scars, as I do, and with creativity and sporting analogies aside, I assert that elemental safety should be our collective pursuit every time. In fact, it shouldn't be an option or a choice, but an absolute right. As I have learned, if it's not evident, walk away.

Our change will generate emotion. At times it may seem as though it's enough to power the national grid. In a highly charged atmosphere, relationships will be put at risk, and environments we once regarded as safe will feel less so. There are two behaviours in particular that often emerge at this time to challenge the safety we once knew, that as leaders we have to deal with.

THE MEETING AFTER THE MEETING

The first behaviour is fragmentation. When as a leader we want people to pull together, they head in the opposite direction. The most visual symbol of this tendency is the 'meeting after the meeting' (MATM), in which after a meeting a reduced set of participants gather to discuss what just happened when everyone was present. This is outside of the beneficial social interaction that often occurs before and after a meeting, and it has a specific purpose. They often occur where insufficient elemental safety has left participants feeling unable to express themselves in the actual meeting. The features of the MATM can be:

- The conversation is likely to be franker and more open
- All participants are de facto within an inner circle, and so feel special
- All participants are there because they want to be, or feel it's necessary
- There's more chance for each participant to speak, due to reduced numbers and the air of confidence from being included
- There's more likelihood of each participant having influence
- Decisions are more likely to be binding, as trust in the smaller select group is stronger
- There's no time limit as no one booked it, so attendees stay as long as they need or can
- They're informal, and so language will be more natural as participants are less likely to be performing and positioning
- There's no formal record of the meeting – it never happened

With the exception of the last bullet, they have all the characteristics of meetings we'd generally prefer to be involved in. Perhaps sometimes also the last bullet. Some participants won't be aware of the damaging nature of such gatherings, or the part in them they're playing. Our solution in times of change is therefore better meetings. And not in times of change, too. As leaders we have to make sure no one feels the need to have the MATM. It just becomes *the* meeting.

LOBBYING

The second behaviour, dating back to common practice at the medieval royal court, is lobbying. Instead of the ear of the monarch being sought, it's the attention of those with power or influence. Lobbying has the potential to open up additional channels of persuasion during times of significant change. As long as we have created suitable, operable and fair channels already, all attempts at lobbying should be closed down.

Often this presents difficulties when leading change where those lobbying are more senior than we might be. The pressure being applied is unfair at best. In such cases the governance structures created (see Part Three) should be sufficient to address any attempt to leverage or persuade. In such instances those lobbying should know better. Yet knowing better and doing better can become separated when there is much at stake. It's here that the practice teeters on the edge of integrity.

As we've seen, however, change challenges trust at every turn. As leaders we have to ensure it doesn't just survive but thrives.

RESOURCES

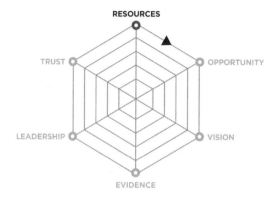

We're at our final component of the operating system. It's at this point that we're tempted to think about a 'journey.' Having readied ourselves we just need to pack for the haul. It may be noticeable that I've avoided the metaphor so far.

Yet this isn't like a yomp across open countryside; we're not considering a static landscape with our only concerns being the unpredictable weather and temperamental livestock. Nothing is standing still. Our resources therefore need to be able to cope with this perpetual movement and the uncertainty it generates. We'll consider primarily those resources we need to organize and bring to us. Some we'll touch on lightly, with a deeper focus on our plan.

PEOPLE

We're highly unlikely to be doing this on our own. One thing we'll have established early is that change is no one's and yet everyone's job. No one's because there is rarely a natural 'department of change' within an organization (unless one has been specifically created, which is still rare). There's no default change function. HR are regularly gifted a barrow-load of expectation because they 'deal with people' but that's unfair because, to varying degrees, we all do. There's little in a standard

HR manager or director job role that suggests they should be responsible for leading all (or even some beyond their own) change within an organization. It's everyone's responsibility because, as we've established, we're all first leaders of change, and then professionals in our chosen field.

There's considerable material available on context-free team composition. We've already considered the part played by trust and elemental safety. Approaches that advocate, for example, 'hiring for attitude and teaching the rest' (usually accompanied by a stock photo of a deliriously happy, carefree young person waiting to learn some stuff), ignore the fact that teaching (and more importantly, learning) takes time and may or may not be successful, because of either our teaching, or the recipient's absorption. Our change initiative may not leave us with the luxury of time and patience. We may also not have the teachers and mentors available with the requisite time available for those with no domain experience at all.

Without this book being able to devote itself to hiring decision theory and practice, suffice to say balance on the team is usually required, relative to the challenge ahead:

- Diversity of, among other things, character, origin, gender, background, life choices and approach – as homogeneity rarely benefits anyone
- Appropriate skills and experience
- A positive and open-minded attitude
- Preparedness to learn
- A willingness to impart useful experience to others at the outset and as it's gained (a rare thing indeed) – so others may learn
- A mix of internal (who understand the organization) and external (who don't) participants and advisors

Much is also made of 'fit.' That is, our judgment as to whether someone will be similar enough in approach, character, personality or skill sets to assimilate without any special effort needing to be made on their or our own part. It's always a judgment call. Yet usually just *enough* fit is all that's needed. I've assembled teams where fit was expected and didn't happen and not expected yet blossomed. I've also led teams where fit was thought necessary yet where in practice it didn't matter a jot, and where it seemed not to matter yet turned out to be important. It's not something for us to get hung up on. Generally, as with most things, we need to avoid the extremes. We'll invariably be surprised.

What matters just as much as the selection of individuals are the relationships that emerge. That is, what happens when we recruit individuals and put them all together. In terms of our role in this, we covered much of what it means in the chapter 'Leadership.' Yet we can't and shouldn't micromanage it all. Much of the time we set the tone and pattern and our colleagues take it from there, as we get out of the way. Sometimes it'll work out, sometimes not, however much we try. The important thing here is that we need to make the call early enough. If a team doesn't instinctively *feel* like it's working, it's probably not. A remedy will be required. That could be down to us, or them. Or both.

ADMIN

It's worth at this point mentioning an often-overlooked or down-played aspect of our initiative – administration. It's often passed over in favour of the more obvious resources needed. There will be more of it than we ever imagine at the outset. However self-sufficient we think we are, we won't be self-sufficient enough. There will be events, gatherings, people, travel, records, actions, prompts, agendas, catering and publications among other things.

While we've focused heavily in this book on the need for the best possible leadership, all leaders will depend on efficient, effective and proactive admin. That's not the same as *an* admin, an assistant – as in, a person. We're (hopefully) well beyond the days of a leader needing someone to dial their phone for them in order to reinforce their status. The admin task might be fulfilled by several people operating in different areas at different phases of the project. Suffice to say it's needed, the challenge will be significant, and a lack of readiness to meet it could be existential. To fail under the weight of overwhelming minutiae would be a tragedy. We should make sure we're ready at the earliest opportunity.

CASH

This book can't advise how we obtain funding for the change initiative in each instance but there are a couple of observations that are relevant. The first is that most organizations create procedures and rules designed to *stop* people spending, irrespective of the value it may create or deliver. Trust is low by default when it comes to parting with cash. That's what we'll be facing. Everyone is assumed to be profligate until proven otherwise. Granted, every organization will need to balance priorities and allocate the scarce resource that money is, but we need to bear in mind that there's every chance that obtaining funding will take longer than anticipated and that which is made available may well be less than requested. There may be science behind the decision; it may just as well be arbitrary. We therefore need to be attuned to less and later, and plan accordingly. We also need a thought as to what to do if it's denied altogether.

Second, as our change initiative started before we thought it did and will go on longer than we think it will, our budget shouldn't be hard-bookended either. We need to ensure that it's sufficient for feasibility (before), contingency (during) and run-on (after). The initial period after we think the initiative has completed can't be barren. It's also a good idea for us to be clear about the funding for run-on, rare as it is to see it in a budget. It's not something to be hidden, but openly declared and thereafter protected. No budget is ever safe, and the less specific components are usually the most at risk.

These considerations aside, we don't always need money, at least not vast sums of it, to make change happen. It can seem that our ability to think creatively is inversely proportional to the amount of money available. The more compelling the vision, the more we're likely to not be dissuaded by a lack of funds. It sharpens our sense of purpose and channels our motivation. When faced with the prospect of the change not happening, or not as we've envisaged or described, we find both ways and means. We're forced to be resourceful and creative – like *The A-Team* (it's an age thing).[69]

GOVERNANCE

We could look at governance here. Like many aspects of the book, they could probably fit into more than one area. Instead, I've left this to the next part of the book, and 'Element 4: Structure' in the chapter 'I'm engaged.'

THE PLAN

There's a comforting certainty in a straight line. We usually can't draw one unaided, but we love to see them. Almost every book about change follows a similar linear path, from initial idea to a new reality shaped by the change.

Plans usually start (and often remain) as straight lines. They're punctured by events significant enough to warrant a mention or to be attached to a person or group. These events are 'phase gates' through which we intend to pass only once. The rest can't happen if we don't. This then becomes a 'critical path' (the shortest possible route from start to finish, with all necessary steps taken). Project planning tools and applications are modelled accordingly. The absence of a plan is in most cases seen on a scale from misplaced confidence to irresponsibility. In such instances blame usually lands upon implementation because it's the stage at which the lack of planning finally becomes visible.

Yet there are drawbacks. They often assume that we'll have everything we need before we start (we don't), that nothing will change en route for the better or worse (it will), that we won't think of something else that causes us to re-evaluate our approach (we will), that everyone involved understands it (they won't) and that the plan is individual-independent (it isn't). The more we invest in the planning process, the more we instinctively trust it. Often, we do so in the face of emergent conflicting information or misinterpretation. The relationship is rarely proportional.

LINEAR STRUGGLES

Some even argue that time itself is non-linear and not the one-way street we perceive. 'Entropy' is a term used in physics that when applied to the everyday world means the gradual decline into disorder.[70] The past to us has far less entropy as we can know and order it, the future significantly more with its almost endless possibilities. In thinking of time as non-linear, we struggle hugely with considering that what may happen in an entropic future may influence the relatively constant present. We struggle too with what we consider to be a static, objective past. It all makes planning rather problematic. This alone goes a long way in itself to explaining why leading change is incredibly difficult.

Time causes havoc. Take the mathematical challenge of dynamic resource allocation.[71] Human beings and systems can solve complex resource challenges comparatively easily, until we introduce the factor of time. Suddenly, the comfortable linearity of planning is out of the window. We need to calculate how to get the right stuff to the right place when needed. Not in a stable, predictable environment but amid the chaos of the world as it's becoming.

All of which serves to challenge our innate draw to linearity. We see a plan as defensive, promoting security, a bulwark against a chaotic world. Irrespective of the effort invested in our plan, however, we'll loop: we'll pass through the same gates more than once (sometimes recognizing them, sometimes not); we'll try to pass through the gates in the wrong sequence; and we'll buck (if not buckle) the critical path with temporary fixes where expedient. We create our own chaos by planning in a linear fashion while behaving in a non-linear way. All the while we still see ourselves adhering to a linear path as a reassuring model we can understand and rely on.

AGILE PLANNING

Planning for change is a soft skill in that it needs to absorb pressure, rather than deflect with its brittleness. Several decades ago, huge IT projects often failed with a depressing regularity. Each phase of activity was completed at scale, to perfect linearity and often over many years. A failure within any of the phases inevitably meant a failure of the whole programme. There was no room for the dynamic and unpredictable to be recognized and incorporated, and for the plan to quickly adapt to new information, developments or circumstances.

In response, in 2001 a group of enlightened software developers produced the *Manifesto for Agile Software Development*,[72] an approach that has since become universally accepted in this sphere, and accidentally spawned multiple uses of the term 'agile.' As a methodology it's also found its way into corporate functions and even entire organizations. It turns out that it's not just useful for software, because it moulds far more to the way we actually work and the entropy ahead.

One of the four pillars of the Manifesto is "Responding to change over following a plan." While there's merit in the latter half of the statement, greater value is attached to the first half. One of the 12 principles of the Manifesto further states: "Welcome changing requirements, even late in development. Agile processes harness change for the customer's competitive advantage." The Manifesto addresses, embraces and embodies change. It's entirely at ease with it and sees it as an integral part of the process, not as something separate or threatening.

That's not to say at all that 'tribes,' 'scrums' and 'sprints' are for everyone. In leading change, it's the level of comfort with change itself at the heart of a soft, adaptive plan that's important. We may sketch our plan in a linear fashion to begin with, that's natural. Thereafter, it needs to absorb, bend and curve, take on information and discard it, see gates as revolving doors. It needs to be comfortable with uncertainty as an inevitability, and an important creator of energy and bearer of insight. Not an inconvenience, deflection or distraction. It must remain a living thing throughout the initiative. We never file away a soft plan.

MEMORIES OF OUR FUTURE SELF

We mustn't forget that we're a resource, too. Just not as we may immediately think.

Our future self is annoying. They're on the other side of the brick wall now in front of us. They've solved the problems we seem to find intractable. They're having a relaxed conversation with friends over a cup of tea saying "Remember the time we couldn't fix that? We never thought we'd be here, did we?" They tell their story with ease. There's no entropy in the future they inhabit. They're on board with non-linear time.

Borrowing from our future self is our own little experiment in chronology. While in turn I borrowed the title for this section from the American singer Reggie Watts (his Twitter bio used to say "We are living in the memories of our future selves"), the philosopher Nietzsche recognized it when he said: "It is our future that lays down the law to our today."[73] It's a simple yet incredibly effective technique. There's no science to it. It's purely a case of drawing down the resourcefulness needed from the trust that there's always a way through, around or over the brick wall – essentially because there has to be. Nothing is ever unsolvable; the future is a myriad of possibilities. I read once in a discussion forum comment, the source since lost and which itself may have been borrowed, the notion that "to predict the future based on the past is imprisonment." We're manifesting the present based on the future.

We borrow in two ways, the cautious and the heroic.

Starting with the latter, an oft-quoted phrase from these quarters is Marshall Goldsmith's (if indeed he originated it) book title *What Got You Here Won't Get You There*.[74] That's only partly right. What got us here was a whole interplay of resources, knowledge, insight, problem-solving, experimentation, courage, unashamed luck and a whole lot more. Getting here was quite a challenge, not to be downplayed. It's one half of the equation. It'll probably get us further. But for the business bookstand it's the half that's not enough. Yet we seek out our careful, calm, wagon-circled future self for reassurance that technically and capably, we did it.

Then there's the aphorism beloved of every self-proclaimed disruptor at which we hinted in the chapter 'Vision,' Henry Ford's "If I had asked people what they wanted, they would have said faster horses."[75] This is the other half, the opportunity-oriented chaos-embracing hero-casting inspiration, the leap into the unknown. It's the stuff of that which gets us there, where the vision lies and where our future self is feet up, regaling with stories of the struggle. We borrow courage from our future self too: we know it made some tough decisions to get there. We know it wasn't always popular, but we're sure it was vindicated.

So, we balance what got us here and what'll get us there. Balance isn't a compromise or a settlement; it's a necessity. By drawing the future back to the present, we make it a shade more possible. We give ourselves the best chance of it being the reality. It fuels optimism and belief. When we reflect on this in the present, the extremes of stultifying caution or unhinged recklessness are, for a change initiative, potentially fatal. It's a choice we don't need to make. Our future self didn't.

OTHER RESOURCES

This chapter might potentially disappear over the horizon. There are many other resources that, as change leaders, we shall need to draw on. That they've not been included here doesn't mean they're not valid.

We could consider existing organizational infrastructure including, tools, processes, methods, systems, technology and physical space. We could stretch this to include culture, attitudes, values (as we covered in Part One), norms of behaviour and documented principles to which we sign up as a result of working for the organization. We could also extend the boundaries of our definition of those resources directly involved – for example, we could include people we're reliant upon complying with and supporting the change initiative but not directly involved. Yet while we draw upon these resources, our task is to navigate them to our advantage. Preferably without draining or diverting them. They'll have other demands on them in addition to those from us.

Wherever we consider the cut-off between those resources we need to organize and those we need to navigate, it's not something to quibble over. We just can't do it all on our own.

RESOURCE MAPPING

It's useful at the earliest stage possible to create a resource map – another living entity that will adapt with the initiative. It may seem like an obvious suggestion, but I can count on the fingers of no hands the amount of times I've seen one. The budget is often considered to be such, but it's not the most appropriate tool for ensuring what we need is available and in place. We need to think more fully than simply creating a list. A suggested framework would answer each of these questions for every resource required – a table too large for the scale of this book:

- What we'll need
- Why we'll need it
- How much/many we'll need
- When we'll need it
- When we'll need to start acquiring it
- How we'll get it
- What happens if we don't get it
- Are there alternative sources?

There we have it – an opportunity to be first.

OUTPUTS AND MEASUREMENT

We have our six components of the operating system of change. Each has identifiable outputs, which may evolve over time, too.

As we move from the generic description of each component of the operating system to the specifics of our initiative, it's incredibly helpful to identify how much we need of each, where we're at with getting there, and the gap we have to close in each case. Otherwise we may just be waving a hopeful finger in the air. Our initiative is likely to demand and deserve better.

It was suggested at the outset that we can use the spider chart for measurement. We can ascribe values, whether qualitative, relative and assessed by us, or quantitative and verifiably measurable by us or others. We can choose how scientific we want to be, albeit the outputs are key in regard to meaningfully mapping our progress.

Figure 23 shows indicatively what an assessment of a pre-initiative position may look like:

FIGURE 23

We may then sketch out where we'd like to be in order to effectively deliver our change initiative. We can choose to map our interim steps, too. Importantly, our targets will invariably either equate to or sit outside our existing position, so the target mass when we join the dots will be greater than the initial state (Figure 24).

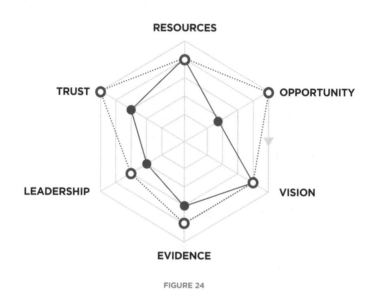

FIGURE 24

Measurement will be particular to our initiative, organization and preferences. There are some usable possibilities related to what we have covered during Part Two, suggested and summarized in Table 8:

COMPONENT	OUTPUT	MEASURE
OPPORTUNITY	Opportunity map	Degree to which is complete – captured fully and meaningfully? Revalidated against the vision?
	Opportunity evaluations	Degree to which is complete – identified key opportunities and maximization plan?
	Risk evaluations	Degree to which is complete – identified key risks and mitigation plan?
	Size of the 'ask' evaluation	Degree to which ask tested (team, peers and those who may be familiar with the organization and/or the nature of the challenge)?
VISION	Message house: vision	Degree to which vision (question) is complete – and is coherent, clear and able to stand scrutiny?
	Message house: objectives	Degree to which objectives are complete, clear and able to stand scrutiny?
	Message house: proof points	Degree to which proof points are identified?
	Message house: approval	Accepted within our governance structure(s)? (See Part Three)

COMPONENT	OUTPUT	MEASURE
EVIDENCE	Data plan: questions	Know what questions we need to answer and why?
	Data plan: collection	Know what we need to collect and how – and if we need technology, what?
	Data plan: analysis	Know who will be undertaking the analysis – and if we need technology, what?
	Data plan: action	Ready, resourced and able to take action if required?
	Story plan: awareness	Team and organization aware of the importance of stories?
	Story plan: collection	Stories available that can support the aims of the initiative – and have they been recorded?
	Story plan: resource	Process for identifying and telling stories as they emerge during the initiative?
LEADERSHIP	Leadership and management structure	Structure in place for the initiative – with no gaps?
	Leadership roles	Leadership roles clearly defined – and a plan in place to fill the roles?
	Leadership behaviours map	Positive behaviours of the leaders appointed evident – and a plan to close any gaps identified?

COMPONENT	OUTPUT	MEASURE
TRUST	Trust assessment	Hurley model to assess whether trust exists in initiative leadership team – and a plan to close any gaps identified?
	Trust survey	Survey to establish levels of trust in organization – and a plan to close any gaps identified?
	Elemental safety assessment	Focus groups to establish whether elemental safety exists (think/feel/act) – and a plan to close any gaps identified?
RESOURCES	Resource plan	Resources required identified and plan in place to obtain them – and all included in budget?
	People plan	Right people identified, roles agreed and ready to fill?
	Budget	Budget prepared and approved – with contingency and run-on?
	Governance units	Structure, governance units and people in place, with clear remit?
	Initiative plan	Flexible, adaptable plan prepared and agreed by governance units?

TABLE 8

We may well be pushing the boundaries of the spider chart with our readiness. However, before we consider what we're going to do, there are some notes of caution.

CAUTIONARY TALES

Our operating system, while logical and comprehensive, faces some naturally-occurring challenges.

FAULT LINES

In Part One we mentioned the inevitable intrusion of the macro-environment in which we'll be operating. We'll also inevitably be facing organizational fault lines with four things: technology, process, activity and communications. They're often out of kilter with one another, to add to the complication.

Technology fault lines can be general, relating to the overall approach, respect for its contribution, commitment to financing, competence to operate, trust in its viability and reliability, future proofing, availability and support. They can be specific, concerning investment (or not) in the necessary hardware, applications or services in areas that will directly impact our initiative. With every organization now to some degree a technology organization, the risk of multiple fault lines is significant. The security risks posed by applications on the face of it harmlessly operating in the cloud means ever-increasing scrutiny and governance further likely to impede progress.

Process covers the ease (or otherwise) of getting things done: policies and procedures, budgeting, approvals, orders and payments (to name a few). Many will be interfaces ('touch points') in our change initiative. They're invariably designed to protect narrowly defined risks or to close rarely detected loopholes, and so usually mitigate against speed and almost never offer a fast lane. They're also usually more vulnerable to the influence of politics and competing agendas than they are open to worthy initiatives.

Activity refers to everything else going on at a given time. We're not operating in an organizational vacuum. There are likely to be other 'process improvement' projects running at the same time as we're planning to implement our initiative.

They may either complement or conflict with what we're trying to do. Much of this activity will be valid and necessary. If they're complementary, we can share the energy and momentum (if allowed). If they compete, it could be directly or simply for time, attention or resources. In such instances personal agendas will, too, as there may be a great deal at stake, from credibility to reward. Almost all organizations are prone to the cult of 'busyness.' Everyone is targeted with achieving something and being able to demonstrate that they have in order to prove their value, and so initiatives proliferate. There is often a benefit to the originator in avoiding integration with other initiatives that might dilute the visibility of their own.

It's this proliferation that gives rise to the notion of 'change fatigue.' Our colleagues become exhausted and disillusioned with the barrage of simultaneous projects, the crossfire of messaging and the cumulative learning burden. Ours may just add to it all. In the practical and emotional tangle of initiatives, we can't assume people will behave and respond rationally. It may appear at times to be a common-sense vacuum. We may therefore need to consider our timing if that's at all optional.

Communication features in Part Three as one of the three groups of elements of change, but here we're concerned with the communication we *don't* initiate or control. We'll be looking at our tone of voice and lexicon, our delivery and interaction media, yet it can be like crossing a California freeway blind-folded and carrying a large tray of drinks, given everything else being communicated at the same time. We'll have to vie for attention with urgent and important messages as much as stuff we don't feel warrants priority. It could relate to that competing activity or just be the daily carnival of corporate noise and interference.

We need to recognize and know the fault lines and develop strategies to work with and around them. We must be street smart. We don't want to be in the position of having to make excuses later.

BOUGHT IN, SOLD OUT

Almost every change book or feature mentions 'buy in.' It frequently crops up in corporate yammer. Yet there's something fundamentally amiss with it.

Thinking in transactional terms is often convenient for us. It's a format we instinctively understand. In this regard, change is seen as a process of moving as many people as possible from 'debit' (sceptical, doubting) to 'credit' (agreeable, convinced) in the balance sheet. The degree – from reluctant acquiescence to unbridled enthusiasm – isn't important. It's the beans in the column. It's thought that some are already in the credit column waiting for us, wondering what took us so long to work it out. Some have set up camp in the garden of belligerence, waiting for us to goof it up or give up. Most are somewhere hovering around the sceptical lobby waiting for something compelling or the twang on a personal nerve that will tip them over.

We call the transition in this instance 'buy in,' as though the purchaser has parted with something tangible in exchange for supporting the change. The implicit notion is that once they're in the credit column they won't be going back – there are no refunds. It's usually deemed a once-only one-way move.

Yet buy in is a misleading idea for several reasons.

First, it's by no means fixed when achieved. We don't glue people into the credit column. The dynamic of change and the influences upon it will invariably lead to a questioning of commitment at some point, if not many. There's just as likely to be buy out and back again, potentially many times. The winning of alignment or agreement is always temporary and subject to reversal.

Second, it's often not a fair transaction. If the proposed change has a negative impact on the recipient, they may be asked to agree to it for broader aims, possibly even the survival of the organization. In such instances buy in means we invest heavily with little discernible return, feeling as though we have to. This leads to an emotional deficit. There's little likelihood of the change being deep and lasting. There is, rather, a significant chance of emergent bitterness.

Third, there's often an actual trade, rendering the change merely a negotiated settlement. It may not involve horses but there may be enough to quantify the deal, leaving no room for emotional connection or commitment. Straightforward bargaining can be effective and is by no means inherently wrong – *if you agree to change, you'll receive* [*something worthwhile*]. However, the trade may be regarded as a one-off, and when it's done we may just go back to where we were. There may even be an expectation of a further trade.

Fourth and finally, buy in may be seen by the investors as the end of the matter. They may switch off and see it as done. If they're not conscious of doing so, it may lead later to a feeling of having agreed to something that looks remarkably different from what arrived. They may even have forgotten they bought in.

There's a better way to look at moving people to a position of support – **critical participation**. That is, permanently sceptical, yet engaged. Being invited to positively critically appraise creates energy and activity and ensures that a broad quality check accompanies the initiative throughout. It isn't negotiation, it's an open offer to appraise at every step of the way. It's fully in step with an adaptive approach. No ledger in sight.

It makes it harder work for us, as time will need to be spent listening to and addressing observations and concerns. There are distinct advantages, though: the chances of groupthink are significantly reduced. By clearly indicating a respect for the experience, knowledge and contribution of our colleagues they'll feel free to offer their views and, without doubt, we'll learn something too. We're building elemental safety. There will be far less chance of our thinking we've won over a group of people who are simply no longer engaged or listening.

As we covered in Part Two, a key aspect of leadership is being confident in asking to be held to account by our team and peers and being similarly confident enough to listen, understand views offered and accept criticism as a gift. Some of what's presented may, of course, be prejudiced, bitter or simply wrong, but we need it all. Our task is to extract the valid contributions, while acknowledging and thanking the time taken for them all.

For everyone involved it'll feel much more like a movement than an accounting exercise. That has to be worth it on its own.

BEING WRONG

At some point, in all probability more than once, it's *going* to go wrong. Yet seeing it as going wrong implies we may have been a victim of a cruel twist of fate and we had nothing to do with it. Chances are at some point *we'll* be wrong. Just us. That may be because of other contributory factors, but our judgment, reading of a situation or instinct will fail us. Given the mesh of interface and dependency that comprise a change initiative, it's a question of to how many times can this be limited.

Two related things are important – to get used to it without welcoming it and to be honest when we do. On this basis the latter will ensure the former doesn't habituate. We really don't want to be admitting *again* that we messed up. Or hunting for excuses or for something or someone else to hold responsible. As the leader of the initiative, it's us.

We must therefore own up when it's us and own it when it's one of our team and protect them. If the error was a result of negligence on the part of a colleague or was the latest in a succession, we may have a management task to perform. If not, we should accept the fallibility of the human condition, jointly understand the situation that arose, learn from it and move on. Their loyalty will take the shape of greater diligence next time.

We'd like to be treated this way, too.

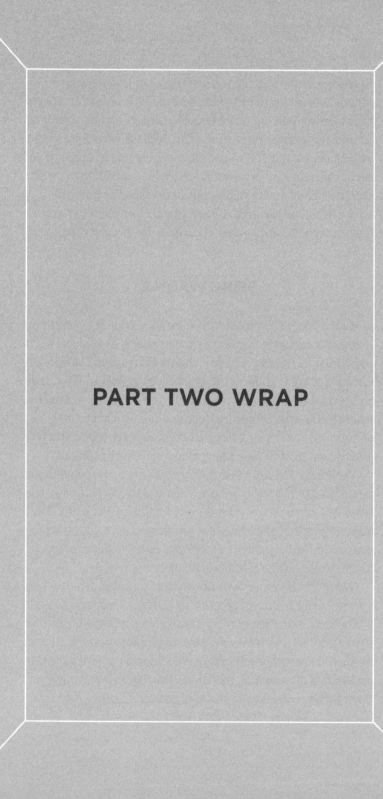

PART TWO WRAP

Here are a few points to reflect on:

- For every risk there should be an opportunity to explore; for every opportunity, a risk to manage.
- We're the easiest person to convince. We should never judge people by our own commitment. What's important to us may not be to anyone else.
- We shouldn't tell people about our dream and ask them to follow it. We should ask them to dream and tell us about it. We share the vision.
- To obtain useful data, we need to ask great questions.
- Stories are parcels of culture. We must send and receive them.
- Change is led from everywhere. Pushed, pulled, nudged, dragged and cajoled. As leaders, it's not all about us.
- We need to feel safe and be safe to think, feel and act. It's elemental.
- The path is never straight, and we'll pass through gates several times. We should never leave them locked.
- Our future self has cracked the problems we face. They're worth getting to know.
- Just as we can buy in, we can cash out. We're not seeking transactors, but critical participants.

PART THREE

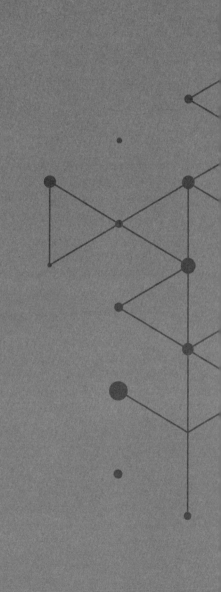

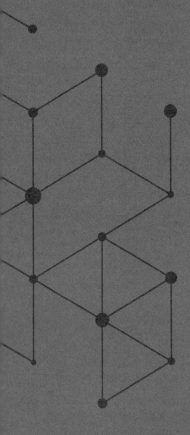

ACTION
WHAT ARE WE GOING TO DO?

THE NINE ELEMENTS
OF CHANGE

It's all very well having a great understanding of change and all the preparation we could wish for, but something has to happen to catalyse it – it's 'what' we do.

There are nine components or 'elements' of the 'what.' They're all needed in our change initiative to some degree. We dial some up and some down as required. It's not a process model with phases or layers or a critical path, nor does it build into a frenzied climax. We don't do one then the other, we're just as likely to consider and start each simultaneously. They're related and each prompts the others.

They're shown in Figure 25 in the form of a periodic table as it's a visual metaphor we recognize. Even if, for those of us who aren't chemists, we don't understand it entirely. In our version, the three-by-three nature reflects a degree of meaningful structure, too.

INFORMED	ENGAGED	INVOLVED
1 **Lx** Lexicon	4 **Sc** Structure	7 **Ps** Presence
2 **Mg** Message	5 **Ep** Example	8 **Av** Activity
3 **Rp** Response	6 **Xr** Exploration	9 **It** Initiative

FIGURE 25

The **columns** – the 'groups' – have the strongest relationship. They comprise three clusters of logically organized activity that have us informed, engaged and involved. Within the column they have similar 'chemical behaviours' which for our purpose means they have a direct relationship.

The origins of this trinity are so deep in the mists I doubt anyone could lay claim to them. That's because it's remarkably simple: we think things, we feel things and we do things. It's always been this way, however evolved our consciousness and faculties. It's how we have developed as a species, all three working in sync. It's an approach that has been used in many guises across multiple disciplines. I've tried to shape and adapt it, making it broadly relevant to change of any form, scale or urgency.

We need all three groups. If we're just informed and not engaged, we don't care. If we don't care, we're unlikely to do anything, unless it's disruptive (not in a tech start-up kind of way). If we just do things without listening or understanding, we're not evolving as we've no basis for why we're doing it, it's meaningless. If we're just engaged, we'll likely be an overemotional mess who just gets on everyone's nerves for no particular reason.

We often hear about change initiatives needing to 'win hearts and minds.' At a basic level this is along the right lines, just not complete. We have to enlist the rest of our body too, or it's just something being done to us that we may grow to resent. As we've already explored, seeking to 'win' is overly transactional for our purposes.

The **rows** – the 'periods' – reflect a degree of depth in each case, increasing as we move down the table. It should be noted that their relationships are more tenuous than the columns and should be treated lightly when considering them together.

The three groups are laid out in Figure 26.

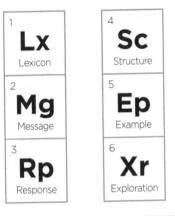

	1 **Lx** Lexicon	4 **Sc** Structure	7 **Ps** Presence
	2 **Mg** Message	5 **Ep** Example	8 **Av** Activity
	3 **Rp** Response	6 **Xr** Exploration	9 **It** Initiative

	I'M INFORMED	**I'M ENGAGED**	**I'M INVOLVED**
GROUP			
BASIS	Factual	Emotional	Practical
PROCESS	Cognitive	Affective	Behavioural
INPUTS	Evidence (data and story)	Perspectives (views and reactions)	Experiences (shared activity)
OUTPUTS	I know ... ... what's happening ... why it's happening ... what it means for me	I feel ... ... inspired ... included ... supported	I will ... ... take responsibility ... be prepared to help ... be prepared to change
BEHAVIOURS	Listening Understanding Asking	Critiquing Suggesting Designing	Volunteering Acting Creating

FIGURE 26

There are some overriding ideas that cover all three groups before we look in detail at each.

THE POWER OF THREE

Three is balance. There's a Latin phrase *omne trium perfectum* appearing to date from the time of Cicero (the first century BCE) that means "everything that comes in threes is perfect." Strangely, it's quite a popular phrase to tattoo. Who knew? The triangle is nature's most robust shape; its inherent rigidity prevents it being crushed. When giving reasons, we often instinctively reach for three. It's the smallest number of units needed to form a pattern. We get brevity and impact, and an ease of recall.

Three is all-pervasive. There are far more examples of common three-point refrains than I can list here, but consider – why, how and what; blood, sweat and tears; faith, hope and charity; life, liberty and the pursuit of happiness; gold, silver and bronze; beg, steal and borrow; red, amber and green (how many times have we assigned RAG status in a list?). There are also the three billy goats gruff, three wise men and three musketeers (although we've all struggled to explain d'Artagnan). The pattern, to a pattern-seeking species, is reassuring.

Comedians often use the approach. Story lies at the heart of their method, and so this links with what was covered in Part Two. We sometimes forget within the gazebo of corporate seriousness that comedians are some of the best communicators we encounter. They don't just tell us stuff; they make it resonate. We're also compelled to share what we find funny, so what they say has a viral potential. As a technique, having created comfort with points one and two they spring a surprise or an absurdity into the third point to create the humour. It's often slightly surreal, and usually makes us feel uncomfortable. Brian Clark quotes just such an example from comedian Laura Kightlinger: "I can't think of anything worse after a night of drinking than waking up next to someone and not being able to remember their name, or how you met, or why they're dead."[76] In the same vein, Neil Mullarkey, communication coach, makes an excellent point on his website when he says: "In business there is no script, every conversation with colleagues and clients is to some extent an improvised scene."[77] Three helps us improvise.

The power of three is therefore standard-procedure marketing. It provides choices, but not too many so as to confuse or disorient. When we take options to leadership for a decision, we often have three: one we recommend (and want), a fallback (we can just about live with, at a push, we'll manage our own disappointment) and a doozie, the one we fear, in there to create balance but we hope doesn't get chosen. It's why our message house has three columns beneath the vision, each with a memorable anchoring idea. It's why our nine elements of successful change are in a three-by-three table.

As a leader, we need to think in threes at every step: talk in threes, engage in threes and involve in threes. It's too firmly founded, too robust and too certain to ignore. Think three choices, three reasons, three advantages, three risks, three stages, three key people. Three. Always. Works.

THE EFFICACY OF HONESTY

Transparency and openness are vital in leading a change initiative. Five years ago, I probably wouldn't have thought to include this short section, but in broader circles than our own it's been somewhat under attack, reduced to relativism. There have been passages of history before our own where facts have been collectively underplayed, ignored or discredited for dubious ends. Our appetite for ignoring facts and truth has in the past only lasted so long before returning out of sheer necessity, and we can only hope so this time, too.

The temptation to skew (or skewer) the truth, underplay or overplay facts or events to create a misplaced emphasis, or withhold information during a change initiative is very real. When we've run the story in our mind, we've inserted the corrective action we'll take to make any transgression or deviation right. The realignments, revelations or balance allow us to rationalize the steps we took. Yet only we or our close associates know the whole story. Our colleagues are at the time blind to the dishonesty and that's something we have to be comfortable with. Fortunately, most of us aren't, even for a moment.

We're often bound up in the utilitarian conundrum – that an action that may be considered in objective terms harmless, albeit not strictly honest, may benefit the greater number. Or caught in a moral judgment that the truth will add little benefit but will inflict hurt, so best it's not disclosed. In these instances, we may consider we're being a good leader when we're actually exceeding our remit – which stops at honesty. In the children's animation *Ben & Holly's Little Kingdom*, the dextrous Wise Old Elf, constantly called upon to repair the chaos caused by the Fairies, consistently decries that "Magic always leads to trouble!"[78] As does dishonesty of any form.

We should also distinguish here between lies and bullshit.[79] Admittedly, it's a thin line. We've always had bullshit, but we've become super-aware of its encroachment into mainstream political dialogue in recent years. With lies we know the truth and decide not to use it. It's conscious deception. With bullshit we don't know the truth and so offer something, anything, with a masking air of authority. As it's a punt, there is a horrible chance it could actually turn out to be right. This just fuels the temptation, as a win might for a gambler.

Alberto Brandolini's *Bullshit Asymmetry Principle*[80] suggests that "the amount of energy needed to refute bullshit is an order of magnitude bigger than to produce it." That could apply to lies too. Lies and bullshit are both exhausting and drain energy and credibility from the initiative. We must avoid them at all costs. And if we don't know, we mustn't bullshit: we should say we don't know and commit to finding out and responding when we do. It's not difficult.

Then there's no guilt, no remorse, no personal compromise, no justification. Honesty is its own reward.

MINIATURIZATION

The small stuff matters. Sometimes painfully, especially when it accumulates.

The expression "don't sweat the small stuff" has been awkwardly misinterpreted over the years. Richard Carlson's book *Don't Sweat the Small Stuff ... and It's All Small Stuff: Simple Ways to Keep the Little Things from Taking over Your Life* from 1998[81] was intended to help us avoid worrying about, and fixating on, things that didn't matter. I can personally admit to a tendency to catastrophize when tired or stressed or both. For instance, I find someone looking at me while I'm signing a form and so the logical thing I'll assume will happen is they'll find out who I am, hack my bank account, forge my signature, steal all my money and leave me homeless and penniless and my wife and children will never speak to me again. And even my hungry dog will hate me.

Instead, the phrase has been cited in many instances to mean the details don't matter so much, they're a distraction for the vision and the grand plan. Detail is so often the key to the success of the change initiative. Yet we're constantly told to see the 'bigger picture' or '80/20' to which most people ascribe their own convenient meaning, not the actual one.[82] For many, change initiatives migrate from the macro to the micro at warp speed, missing out many stations in between. While we're careful with our vision question and objectives, it's about *what it means for me*. The miniaturization process often follows a path from the head to the heart, a reverse of much change folklore. We find ourselves suddenly and irrationally caring about things that in the grand scheme don't matter especially. But they matter to *us*.

In one particular change to a radical style of working environment, with a carefully curated design based on workflow and opportunity creation, I observed that the most talked-about issue was that, with teams sharing space, it was difficult to find a stapler. We could have solved that ourselves by buying our own, if it meant that much. But we don't buy our own staplers in offices, do we? For all the investment, thought, energy, commitment and time that went into the project, after months on the hob it all boiled down to the elusive stapler. In this case, an individual paper-affixing unit represented 0.001% of the budget.

What follows from the miniaturization is the explosion. The inability to locate a stapler means that *the whole damn place doesn't work*. First, we take the rational issues down to what it means to us – then, explode them such that the emotion colours everything we see and experience. We actively look at everything as though it won't work, and then find ways in which it doesn't. Of course, it operates the other way, too. If I find a detail works fantastically for me (I can locate a stapler easier than before), then the whole project is *incredible*, the best idea we've ever had.

As we progress, we'll find items and ideas out of place. They'll come to symbolize the entire process of adjustment. Even tidying a room at home has the same effect. Rearranging the contents of the kitchen cupboards may create a much more logical cooking-oriented arrangement, and if we had a brand-new kitchen it might make sense. But things aren't where they used to be. For some time, we spend much longer than we used to looking for things. And we curse a lot.

When raised, the small stuff isn't a cause for irritation but a clear sign that our colleagues are on their way to the desired change. We mustn't dismiss it, but recognize, acknowledge and welcome it. They'll also let us know what's bothering them. As we'll see with communication, closing the loop effectively is incredibly powerful: "You said, we did." As long as we actually do the "did."

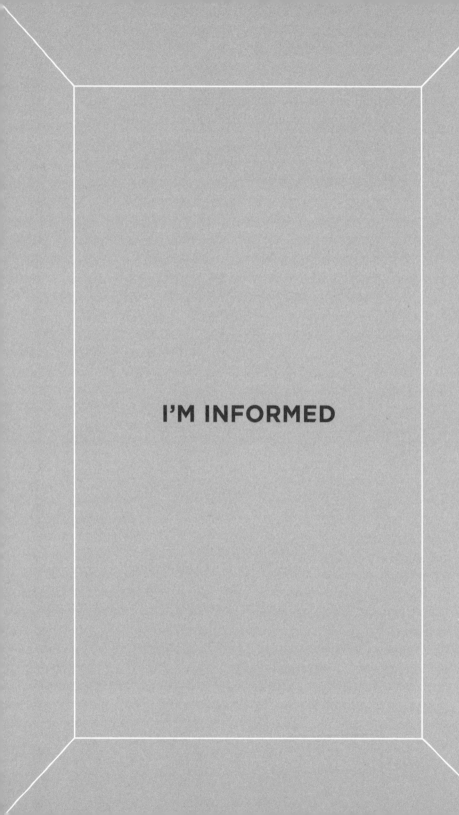

I'M INFORMED

We want – and need – to know what's happening. But not just that. We also need to know why it's happening, how it's going to happen, who's doing what (and to or with whom), when and where it's happening, what it means for me, what I need to do, what happens if it doesn't happen, and what happens if something else happens instead. That's quite a shopping list.

It could be that there have been enough articles featuring 'top ten tips' for effective communication published in recent times. They keep coming, suggesting perhaps we're not listening or processing properly, but it's not as easy as today's lists might make it appear. Of the three groups in our periodic table communication is certainly the most comprehensively addressed elsewhere. This may be because change for many often stops at telling people what's happening. There's no doubt, of course, that it must be done.

Change is often bracketed with communication in budgets and plans, as though it's the only tangible, recognizable and required part of change and so will avoid an unceremonious red strike-through. That still happens all too often, anyway, on the assumption that communication is free.

That said, I've encountered change projects led confidently on an entirely inexplicable 'need to know' basis only, where information was withheld until so late that it was worthless, or restricted until it was leaked – out of sheer exasperation – by the few who knew. I've also been asked (and declined) to 'do the change management' on projects where for no apparent reason all the key decisions had been taken without anyone but the leadership team knowing what was happening.

We're just answering the questions we began this chapter with – before they get asked. We do so by considering the lexicon and tone of voice we use, the message itself and the response it generates.

ELEMENT 1: LEXICON

Taking time to think about the manner in which information will be conveyed is vital. The substance has to be accompanied by style – style not meaning big pointy collars and flares in this sense, but simply a discernible and recognized form. The more down-to-earth and honest our lexicon (the words we use) and tone of voice (how we say them), the more it'll resonate with those affected.[83] They're intrinsically related. We've grouped both for convenience under the first of our choices, lexicon. Mainly because, in its own right, it's an engaging word.

Carefully crafted and edited 'corporate-speak' using a language only heard and read airside of the revolving door can create an instant divide between the tellers (and their cohort) and the told. What we mean by this is words we wouldn't normally use in regular conversation, and sentence construction, that lend themselves far more to the written word than the spoken. A project manager on one of my teams, one of the most straight-talking individuals one could hope to meet, would, when writing 'formally,' find words I hadn't even realized existed – like 'heretofore' – wrapped in convoluted sentences that buckled under their own weight. It was the most extraordinary flip to a style he felt was necessary. In all other scenarios his trusted, direct methods were appreciated by others and served him well enough.

THE WORDS WE USE

First, lexicon – the words we use. The choice of words is, for some, where they first notice that the change process has begun. If we're being spoken to in a different manner, we're more likely to believe that something is happening, or about to. This is particularly so when thinking about the formal and informal. I've seen the power of a simple switch made by an internal service team from referring to fellow workers as 'customers' (the same term as used for those externally buying the organization's products and services) to 'colleagues.' The new term was positively loaded with meaning and connection and instantly began to beneficially change the dialogue and relationship. The service team lifted the targets from their rumps and started taking pride in what they did and the contribution they made. Their colleagues, in turn, respected and appreciated their efforts.

Change is particularly susceptible to our choice of words. Where we use words such as 'resistance' whether intended or not, or even if paired with more positive choices, we begin to create a divisive atmosphere around our initiative. We undermine confidence, sowing seeds of doubt about our vision and its potential to be delivered. We place ourselves firmly on the back foot. Subsequently, getting ourselves off it requires a disproportionate amount of energy.

When we make a conscious decision to change lexicon, in general (but not exclusively) the shift of gear is 'downward' – that is, to a simpler, less formal style (we rarely decide to be more pompous, but, of course, can't rule it out). It feels more natural, and we feel more like we're being trusted with the information given. It can be achieved with just a few words. It doesn't have to be a wholesale switch from BBC English to Cockney rhyming slang in one step, or this just feels too contrived. Our colleagues will wonder what has happened to us. Moving from 'personal possessions' to 'stuff' makes a big enough leap and introduces as acceptable a word most of us use regularly without causing (in the main) particular offence. We all have, use, buy and do stuff. It's naturally associated. The word appears 55 times in this book.

HOW WE SAY THEM

Second, tone of voice – how we pitch the words we use. Using everyday words like an Etonian won't wash, neither will quoting Homer in Greek with the lilt of a Sunday league football coach.

The saggy-chops dog Droopy, created by the Metro-Goldwyn-Mayer studio in 1943, spoke in the same drab monotone from a deadpan face whether ecstatic or apoplectic. That was the comic effect, of course, the complete disassociation of content from tone. It can come through in both spoken and written word. As Alex Lickerman says, "Our tone tells the truth even when our words don't."[84]

So, we need to weave lexicon and tone together into something coherent and congruent such that what we say is noticed. We're creating a lexicon and tone that says *change is happening*. This, against a backdrop where securing our attention under constant content bombardment is ridiculously difficult. It's a hugely competitive field. Worse still, we don't know where we stand relative to the filters applied by our colleagues. So, in our messaging we have to be better, sound better and look better than we ever have before.

It's likely that our new approach isn't entirely natural for us, either because of the way we normally communicate or the way we've trained our self to do so in a corporate environment. We may therefore need to learn the new approach. The lexicon and tone need to be consistent, and so a number of people will have to master it so that it sounds as one voice. It means several of us effectively creating and stepping into a new shared persona.

It's worth underlining that an assessment of the desired lexicon and tone needs to take place at the earliest stages of a change initiative, not halfway down the track when we've already carried on as previous. We need to establish authenticity from the outset. We shouldn't say anything until we know how we want to say it, even when time is pressing. It's often the case that we spend so long talking about what we're going to say we end up in a rush to say it. If we blow it the first time, the second communication isn't a second chance. Especially at the beginning it's worth taking a little longer to get it right even if it means wrestling with a portion of executive impatience.

THE SIGNS AND SYMBOLS WE USE

Not everything we say is with words. Sometimes as leaders of change what we do or create act as signs and symbols. Sometimes we use *actual* signs and symbols instead of words. All can be considered part of the lexicon.

A **sign** stands for something else, tangible or intangible, and accesses a common, shared meaning within a certain culture or area. The level of ambiguity is low, as it *denotes* or *instructs*. A **symbol** meanwhile is a sign that may be open to interpretation even within that same culture. It *suggests*, raising ambiguity levels. Unlike signs, symbols can become their own idea entirely. Those associated with the discipline of semiotics agree on the basic premise that a symbol is a type of sign. Much as I ponder this, it seems the wrong way around.

Recently, our need for brevity-driven forms of digital messaging across a myriad of platforms has caused a huge increase in their use in communication. The emergence of emoticons and emoji could well be down to the rise to almost universal recognition of the Acid House music 'smiley face.' Originally created by American graphic designer Harvey Ross Ball in 1963 for a morale campaign for the State Mutual Life Assurance Company in Massachusetts (what, you've never heard of them?), it took him ten minutes and he was paid $45.[85] Following a period of emergence as a recognizable symbol in several guises it became the music movement's icon in late 1987. This was thanks to DJ Danny Rampling who used it for his new night club, Shoom, borrowing it from Barnzley, the designer at the Wag Club who would wear the symbol on (most of) his clothes.

Emoticons and emoji aren't the same.[86] An emoticon (a mash-up of emotion and icon) is a typographic display of a facial representation used to convey emotion in text only, using punctuation and other keyboard symbols. Like :-). While their use can be traced back as far as 1635,[87] it's highly likely they were in use long before. Unlike emoticons, emoji are actual pictures. They were created in the late 1990s by NTT DoCoMo, the Japanese communications firm. The name roughly translates as 'pictograph.'[88]

In using signs and symbols we need to consider both lexicon (which ones, how appropriate they are to the subject and situation, and the change we wish to convey) and tone of voice (how we use them, where and in what degree). In both respects we need to think through their relationship to the words we use, and why we use them in those instances instead of words.

Clearly, powerful as signs and symbols are, in our role as communicators of change we must be careful with their use. Signs, being obvious, may be too lacking in sophistication, their instructions often brisk, brief and blunt. Conversely, symbols may engage, but risk multiple interpretations. Both are best explained before being able to stand alone (why and what). Thereafter, and used economically and carefully, they achieve the reinforcing character needed, with brevity and theatre.

ELEMENT 2: MESSAGE

Let's consider it's our turn to speak. Most of us enjoy that. There are three questions we need to ask ourselves.

WHY ARE WE COMMUNICATING?

There are several possibilities.

We believe we have something people ought or need to know, such that we *must* say it. In which case we need to make sure it's necessary. Is the 'must' here something that's obsessing us, or is it really as important as we assume?

We could have made a commitment to say something at a particular time or interval, so feel we ought to be saying it. In which case, did we put ourselves under unnecessary pressure?

If our change initiative will last two years, a weekly bulletin may be overdoing it and we'll soon have nothing to add. If we waffle something out at intervals we've determined and there's little to say, our colleagues will soon switch off, even when something finally lands that's important.

It could just as likely be that we haven't said anything for a while and feel we need to. In which case, do we have anything new or has it been a natural break? Sometimes it may be necessary just to let everyone know that there hasn't been any communication recently. Specifically saying there's no update can be entirely valid.

Similarly, we shouldn't always wait until we know everything. If part of a deal or a particular choice remains confidential until signed or finalized, it's OK for us to let colleagues know what we can disclose and reference why we can't detail the rest. Waiting till we can say everything risks frustration on the part of those hanging on in expectation and, in this age of ease of access to information, a leak.

HOW ARE WE COMMUNICATING?

This covers both the manner of communicating (we've already covered the lexicon and tone of voice) and the medium. For communication to be effective, channel and style are inseparable. Using emoticons in a formal memo will feel like dad dancing. Sending a formal memo by social network will make it look and sound like we've been hacked by teenagers.

In terms of channels, it's safe to say there are more than ever available and probably will be even more in the time between my writing and you reading this. The formal may have taken a battering at the hands of internal and external social feeds, but they're still useful at certain times. Very few channels have actually died away in the rush to the new. Yet we still complain about email, and if one channel is destined to be ignored it's that, which has been dominant for a quarter of a century and arguably, despite our best endeavours, still is.

For the written word we now have a choice of dedicated websites (often microsites – discreet groups of pages within a website), enterprise social networks (closed social platforms, often referred to by the acronym ESN – more on these a little later in 'I'm informed: Or am I?'), team-oriented platforms and multiple publicly available social channels allowing private message groups, along with the more familiar email, direct message services and, of course, that old stalwart, paper. One project leader I worked with created quite incredible cohesion and guaranteed her communications would be read and understood by interspersing the use of email and digital channels with personally hand-annotated and signed notes. The colleague group in this case was around 200 people, and so while manageable, it was an effort on her part – but it returned benefit in spades. We 'write off' the traditional methods at our peril.

Delivered-in-person, options include town halls, exhibitions, surgeries and interventions at regular meetings (sales, team, management and so forth). We'll cover these throughout Part Three. When we consider the sheer scale of channels alone, we've little excuse for not reaching our colleagues.

Proliferation may, however, in itself be a problem. We need a consolidated notification feed that makes our exposure to multiple channels manageable. Inevitably, we'll miss things. A technology business I worked with recently were dealing with the hurt of some of its younger colleagues when they missed the anniversary party as the invitation had been routed through one social channel only that they did not use. The non-attendees only realized the party had taken place when they encountered the hangovers of the majority late the next morning. In which case, we need to be clear from an early stage as to which channel will carry what information and stick to it. It presents an opportunity to drive the growth of a preferred yet underutilized channel if it's understood that all the important information will be available there.

WHAT ARE WE COMMUNICATING?

We know that it's worth saying and how we're going to say it. Now we need to establish the content. In crafting it we need to be:

- **Clear**. We should follow the rule of thumb that, no matter how clear we think we're being, we're probably not being clear enough. That will inevitably apply to parts of this book, too, despite what I may consider to be my best efforts. So we must always try to be clearer. An inherent difficulty with judging our clarity is that it's determined by the receiver of the communication, not the creator. It's greatly aided by structure, both for us in preparing it and the reader in finding what they need. We're all check-listing it. The time-honoured approach of "say what you're going to say, say it and say what you said"[89] may help too. It's attracted some criticism in recent years for being unsophisticated, yet it's noticeable how often it still works. It's also worth mentioning the 'serial-position effect' discovered by the German psychologist Hermann Ebbinghaus (he of the 'learning curve') whereby we recall the first (the 'primacy effect') and last ('recency effect') items in a list far more effectively than anything in the middle. So, being especially clear at the beginning and end of what we say is vital.

  Finally, in this respect we should always try to speak as a newcomer to the subject. It helps us avoid being consumed by (often unconscious) assumptions of prior knowledge based on our own familiarities. Jargon and acronyms are usually the worst offenders. Having our communication reviewed first by a trusted soul completely unfamiliar with the subject matter or the initiative can be useful.

- **Straightforward**. Clarity is greatly aided by straightforwardness. You'll notice I didn't say 'simple' as this is too often confused with its ugly sibling, 'simplistic.' While we imagine that the aim of communication is to be understood, we could be forgiven in most instances for assuming that the intention was the opposite. Whether in the misplaced belief (as we mentioned earlier) that we *need* to speak differently in a corporate environment or that big ideas need big words, stating what we mean in an understandable way isn't insulting someone's intelligence. On the contrary, it's respectful. We're acknowledging that time and attention may be limited, and so we're making it as easy as possible to navigate.

Organizing our thinking and communication using interrogative words such as why, how, what, where, who and when is massively helpful both to us and the recipient. The Franciscan friar William of Ockham (*c*. 1285–*c*. 1347) would have approved. He wasn't the first to advocate that more straightforward explanations are preferable to complex ones, but he emerged as the undisputed champion of the cause and had the notion of a 'razor' attributed to him. We use 'Ockham's razor' to shave away what isn't necessary until we arrive at what we need. As with clarity, however straightforward we think we're being, we could probably be more so. We can still use Ockham's razor when we're explaining complex ideas or plans. There isn't a threshold after which we discard the need to be straightforward.

- **Economical**. We should avoid blethering on if we don't need to, even if we're being clear and straightforward. And we'll rarely need to. However economical we think we've been we've probably said too much. In communicating our change initiative, we're rarely engaged in an exercise in literary expression. When we're stuck, verbosity is no hiding place. It's quite possible at times in this book I've gone on too long (and just as likely I've skipped over an important point). We may think it'll make us look grand and give us time to think. Or give us time to think "How the hell do I get out of here?" Our audience will be treated to "verbal overload, value underload" as Arthur Plotnik says.[90] He states, too, that sometimes when the stakes are high, we may expect verbiage.[91] However, if we find that they are, and we feel we must speak, we should use words of high symbolic value to ease the burden on the listener. We shouldn't just waffle, Plotnik asserts, we should make it sound pivotal. Many politicians have heeded this advice.

Being economical takes time and effort, however. As the French mathematician and philosopher Blaise Pascal said in 1657, "If I had more time, I would have written a shorter letter."[92] My personal favourite was from a mammoth 'process re-engineering' (sorting our crap out) slide deck created several years ago by a fast-track management protégé in which he implored us to 'eradicate undue complexity.' Really.

- **Interesting**. Having striven to be clear, straightforward and economical, we need to try to make it worth receiving. Dull is rarely completed. If we've previously been dull, next time it's unlikely to even be started. We may sometimes need to make the mundane but necessary interesting, too. This is where stories are helpful, as we covered in Part Two. We shouldn't overreach in the other direction and try to be dramatic where it isn't warranted. Interest doesn't have to shout.

- **Balanced**. Being even with positive and negative messages is tricky. We shouldn't assume it's possible. The primacy of our emotions means that a negative bias is often evident. If we're told nine good things about our work and one critical thing, we'll likely focus on the critical. We need to take extra care when conveying bad news, and never make it personal or apportion blame. If we're not careful, we can easily undo all our diligent work in building positivity in one go. With the positive, we must be clear on how we sustain and develop it. With the negative, we have to build an achievable path to recovery.

- **Genuine**. We need to ensure we sound natural. We should avoid trying to construct like we *imagine* the corporate communications team would and write as though we mean it.

The output from corporate comms often comes in for criticism. Not because of any lack of knowledge, skill or talent, of which there's often plenty, but because with the multiple hands involved in shaping the content, it can sometimes feel as though it's been pushed through a sieve of policy and guidance to separate it from its soul. We can and should be and sound like ourselves.

- **Inclusive**. We should ensure we always speak to everyone, irrespective of the way they are or the way they choose to be. Even when we're addressing a particular group, we should assume we have no idea of the composition or preferences of the group in case it unconsciously shapes what we're trying to say. The group we're addressing will change, in that some will join, and others will leave. We should also try to avoid the temptation to segment our audience and talk to each group in a different way. It will drive us to make assumptions and generalizations that may well transpire to be wrong. We're all adults and we're fine with being treated that way.
- **Honest**. We covered this in the first chapter of Part Three, under 'The efficacy of honesty.' It's a golden rule. Always.

In Part Two, the importance of **storytelling** was explored. It's quite possible for a story to either achieve all of the above, or to accompany a communication that achieves all of the above as illustration or reinforcement. It's a matter of judgment as to whether, given the reason and timing of the message that needs to be conveyed on each occasion, story is suitable.

By way of an example that draws on several of these themes, working for a company that took health and safety incredibly seriously and that produced more written material on it than I'd ever seen, I inherited a team with a very poor accident and injury record. There was no apparent reason, and the organization's leadership were flummoxed. We were setting a bad example. What was happening was operational staff couldn't find guidance that was clear and relevant to them, so they ignored it all. Instead of issuing yet more material and training, we stripped it all right down to a simple sentence/paragraph/page approach, one that Ryan Holiday has since written about.[93] We ditched the rest. It became simply: *own it, know it, test it, report it, improve it.* We explained each a little more and gave applicable illustrations. We constantly reinforced the five pillars. Accidents declined, and the commitment to safety improved.

BROADCASTING

There's a lot of schtick given in communication advice to broadcasting – telling without any intent to listen or means of doing so. One-way traffic. Yet sometimes we have to. It's a question of knowing when it's necessary. Not all information provided needs to be two-way. Even with communication that allows for a response channel we won't know if it's been consumed or understood. If it's a cast-iron nailed-on date something is going to happen that will affect us, it's not a conversation, it's something we just need to know.

The two keys here are: we need to know when to broadcast, when to communicate; and if the former, be absolutely clear in what we're saying (as we've already covered), or we'll create an unfair expectation of a conversation. In fact, we must be even clearer with a broadcast than a communication and leave no room at all for doubt.

SECOND-HAND NEWS

We should never underestimate the power of informal communication, on two levels.

First, those messages not heard or received by some, where they subsequently rely on the interpretation provided by others. This may happen occasionally: they were away, they missed it, they deleted it. It may also be a carefully crafted habit: they never bother, and always ask someone else.

This isn't always negative, though. Sometimes the clarity of the message may be improved.

The role of the willing interpreters should be acknowledged, those who look out for messages and set about summarizing them for the benefit of others. Whether the others want it summarized or not. These unknown and unsung assistants can do our initiative a grand service and ensure that communication reaches those who otherwise may not have received it or not bothered to have read it. Of course, there will be some who make it worse through their own lack of understanding of the message, their inability to communicate it or just pure mischief. It's the: "Did you see that email from the CEO? Looks like we're all fired at the end of the month." It's always worth asking ourselves how our communication might be interpreted by others, as there's a fair chance of what we conclude actually happening.

Which leads us on to the second, rumours. These emanate either from messages created in the absence of anything provided, or from misinterpretation (deliberate or accidental) of, or extrapolation from, our communication (we said x and therefore y must be true). It may even be a combination. They're guesswork. Rumours can gather a momentum of their own and run entirely wild. An initial error or supposition is enough to generate another, and so on, such that the distance from the truth becomes exponential. Drawing the line under such a threat needs to be done at source or we just end up deadheading plants that keep sprouting and growing. Identifying the origin isn't always easy and can be incredibly distracting and energy-sapping.

We should remember, of course, that – like bullshit, a close relative – rumours can be true. Even the mischievous ones. We might actually all be getting fired at the end of the month. A story will always be told, so best we're telling it. The thing we're least capable of handling, however, is the void. An increase in rumour traffic is usually proportional to the length (time since it was filled) and depth (anticipated consequences of what may be about to happen) of the void. Avoid the void.

NUDGE, NUDGE

Like using metaphors, we 'nudge' more often than we think. It's refreshing to use an easy term. We could call it 'libertarian paternalism' – the name that analysts and academics use to describe it – but life's too short. We're free, but we're being guided as to what (is determined) is best for us. We have a choice, but our brain has been subtly wired, unbeknown to us, to make sure we don't exercise it. Even though we happily think we have.

The theory was first articulated by Richard Thaler and Cass Sunstein in 2008.[94] It starts from the premise that we're not rational. Therefore, helpless creatures that we are, we need some assistance. A nudge guides our choice of behaviour without closing any other options. It's only a nudge if it's easy to take an alternative. Like the famous example of the 'target' fly painted on the men's urinals at Schiphol Airport,[95] which substantially reduced cleaning time and costs. Users of the facility don't have to aim for it, but they generally do.

The key to an effective nudge is a simple, usable default. In choice architecture, as we covered in Part One, we're more likely to choose a default than a deviation. However, the approach does lead to charges of bias, and an ethical doubt that it might be manipulation. The same, however, could be levelled in some form to all approaches to trying to change behaviour.

In leading change, we can't underestimate the power of a simple, accessible and generally sensible nudge. It'll be a time of heightened emotion and greater crackle on the airwaves. Easily navigable compulsion-free decisions that clear the path will help everyone. Once again, however, we need to beware of overuse, as balance is vital. We'll be outed as a schemer if the approach appears dominant, and it'll drive the opposite behaviour. Rebellion, in its own way, prompted by a nudge.

SENSING THE IMPENDING

We're accustomed to change spinning on an axis of communication – verbal, written and graphical. We see and hear the messages given to us and respond in kind. Yet we have five senses. The more we open the channels available, the greater the chance of our need to *experience* change being fully satisfied. After all, we're constantly being told to "wake up and smell the coffee."

The idea of 'experience' has gained significant traction in the post-industrial age. In many areas we've seemingly exchanged the benefits and status of ownership for comparatively fleeting yet far more widely variable stimuli. The idea of 'collaborative consumption'[96] (as in, the 'sharing economy') tells us that usage trumps ownership. We're lighter, more mobile, potentially freer and we've more stories to tell. Yet experience is highly personal. How I perceive a situation or occurrence may vary widely from others in the same space, both directly and due to ideas already covered in this book, notably context and values in the chapter 'Local thinking' in Part One.

The personal nature of experience is precisely why exploring change through the widest sensory palette is both vital and often overlooked. While this is clearly easier in the literal sense when we're, say, renovating a restaurant than introducing a new accounts payable system, it's through communication that we can open as many channels as possible.

There are distinct biological reasons why some less-explored senses in this regard are incredibly important. Our olfactory receptors are linked to our limbic system, the part of our brain that deals with emotions and memory. This means we create lasting recollections through smell that we can't mask or suppress. When I catch a whiff of a particular kind of mint I'm immediately transported to my grandmother's house on the south coast of England, given they could be found in every drawer of the house. At that point I expand the detail of my memory, I'm there in a broad sense. They're lovely memories of childhood.

Beyond the evident sight and sound, through smell, touch and taste we can create associations, meaning and commitment. In turn, this can widen the discussion, adding greater confidence in the communication in both directions. The difficulty is, they're not very 'corporate.' The term 'touchy, feely' is mostly used in a derogatory manner, as though of lesser importance. It's not the chunky, robust stuff of change we're expecting – which is exactly why it should be considered. The tactile, olfactory and gustatory can convey so much more than a bullet point.

We may not always be treated to a broad sensory landscape to guide us along the change path, but we'll sure as heck smell bullshit a mile off.

ELEMENT 3: RESPONSE

Without doubt the process of change must involve two-way communication at various junctures. This implies that one group is talking while the other group is (we hope) absorbing it, clarifying where necessary, processing, understanding – and potentially responding. Offering information only *becomes* communication when it's understood at the receiving end. Yet that event often prompts a response. Intentional broadcast aside, the response needs a channel. Everyone impacted by the change needs to feel as though they have a voice, have been heard and are likely to be heard again when they choose to speak.

As change leaders, we want a response because of one or more of the following:

- We need a choice to be expressed
- We need insight, input or answers
- We want something to be evaluated
- We want a receipt

In regard to a receipt, however, if we're going through the motions, giving our colleagues the impression they're included and involved and just want our message acknowledged, we really need to take a deeper look at ourselves.

If we want a *worthwhile* response, we need to seek it in the best way possible. We can:

- Give information and allow a response, freely or from a list
- Give information and invite comment
- Ask questions and invite colleagues to think about their answers for themselves
- Ask questions and invite answers

ASKING QUESTIONS

All questions aren't equal. There are two traps we need to avoid – loading them, or expressing them negatively and thereby inviting a negative reaction. We're all familiar with loaded or leading questions, like "How brilliant do you think this book is?" We're often less familiar with how a simple change of lexicon, tone or emphasis enable us to ask exactly the same thing but create a positive and fair mindset rather than simply invite criticism.

The Solutions Focus school of coaching, referenced in Part One, is particularly strong on the importance and structure of questions. It's designed to discover what's working to be able to do more of it, rather than define and analyse problems. I'm grateful for the advice of Mark McKergow in this regard.[97] As he points out, we often look to the negative to provide insight hoping that it'll help us to the positive. We can, however, go straight to the positive. When we ask, for example, "What prevents us from conducting a great interview?" it's like going shopping and listing everything we *don't* want. I've known some eccentrics, but I don't think any would lay claim to such a tactic.

RESPONSE CHANNELS

The choice of channels for response must reflect our differences.

We can use public space. Town halls are ideal for (and welcomed by) those with a voice like a foghorn and a confidence to use it, but not helpful for those with less of a propensity to speak openly. They need a channel for a much more personal conversation. Exhibitions (which we'll cover under Element 6) allow selective one-to-one conversations to take place in a more convivial space without time constraint, within reason.

We can use written channels, those covered when we looked at the message in Element 2. The response may be in the form of free expression or controlled in a survey or questionnaire. They may be open and social, or private. It takes a particularly confident culture for matters of any importance or sensitivity to be at ease with relying on open social channels for the response. Even where anonymity is assured it's not always accepted, with a lurking concern that our scathing attack on the organization's strategy might be traceable back to us. A response may not always therefore be offered, either in part or in full. Every organization accommodates a degree of bottled-up anxiety; few offer a genuine elementally safe channel for its expression. It's something we should strive to create.

THE ART AND NECESSITY OF LISTENING

If we're to encourage a response, it follows that we need to listen to it. Kate Murphy in *The Guardian* noted that, "One of the most valuable lessons I learned as a journalist is that everyone is interesting if you ask the right questions."[98] She also adds that while we're often schooled in the art of presenting information, we're rarely taught to listen. We're just expected to know how.

Listening is just as much a skill as creating and delivering messages.

We can do four things to help us develop the skill, to be better listeners. First, show patience, something in increasingly short supply. When we're listening, it's not our turn to speak, nor are we just passing the time waiting for our turn to speak. Second, provide recognition that the voice has been heard, in personal form, not just a receipt. We hate to be shouting into a vacuum as much as staring into a void. If we doubt we've been heard, we just get louder and more frustrated. If we've asked for views or a decision, we need to play it back. Third, filter the signals from the noise. Feedback will contain wisdom and insight, and should be expected to, as there are likely to be great ideas within strands of concern. Finally, watch. Sometimes it's what we don't say that matters. That may simply be stony silence, but invariably feedback will consist of physical cues, too. We don't simply speak with our mouths; we convey as much, if not more, with our facial expression and body language. Unlike language, facial expressions are relatively universal (albeit we can't say the same for gestures).

It's important to note, too, that listening isn't a process of simply receiving information while remaining mute. We're involved. We need to seek clarification, ask further questions, dig into areas of interest. Charles Dickens noted that, "The worst of all listeners is the man who does nothing but listens."[99] We see this occasionally with those training themselves to be better listeners. They try so hard *not* to speak that they don't provide any feedback at all. By taking part we also *demonstrate* that we're listening, which is advantageous to both parties.

If we're using the response to help frame our strategy, if we're mining insight to guide our initiative, and if we can let our colleagues know they've contributed, this isn't only extremely powerful, it may well create a better outcome altogether.

In some of the social channels we referenced earlier in Part Three, the communication loop may move at some speed. Where it's *possible* to respond quickly there's usually an expectation that we *will* respond quickly. Even when using more traditional methods our communication will create dialogue that we'll need to manage. It's important to remember, though, as we stand on the brink of being consumed by it, that the conversation isn't the change initiative. As Jean-Paul Sartre said, "... you have to choose: live or tell."[100] We have to manage the time we invest as much as the filters we apply and the insight we derive.

THE Q&A

While listening is vitally important, we can answer many questions before they're asked. We should have a good idea what they'll be. We've either heard them already or we can place ourselves in the position of our colleagues and imagine what they'll want to know.

We'll need to be detailed and thorough because despite the sense that we're on a one-way expressway to brevity, some people always want to read the terms and conditions. Even when they're printed in light grey text we'd need to be a fly to read, or flash in front of us with a consenting tick-box, not allowing us to use our new application until we've agreed to surrender our neighbour's first born should we transgress. Slight over-exaggeration aside, it means we have to write them and make them available. We'll probably groan at the thought as it's time-consuming, but it's incredibly useful in two respects.

First, we're giving useful form and substance to the conversation, and controlling our responses using the approach we completed earlier in Part Three. We really can try to leave no room for ambiguity.

Second, it also means we have to explain to *ourselves* everything we're doing. As we mentioned in Part One, we're the easiest people to convince that our change is worthwhile. Yet as we work through the detail, we'll realize that we haven't thought of everything, that we took some situations for granted, that we missed some key considerations, and that there are scenarios we still need to plan for. We'll find a whole heap of the small stuff in here too and be able to anticipate the miniaturization about to occur.

We need to start early and grow the material as we get asked more questions as the conversation unfolds. It'll be a living collection. It also means in the long run we'll spend less time responding to the same questions – there will be a return. We'll free the time we would have spent on these matters to allow us to listen to more particular and nuanced issues and concerns. We can't scrimp on this exercise, however tempting.

I'M INFORMED: OR AM I?

We have our lexicon and tone of voice sorted, and our approach to communication – message and response – honed. There are some cautionary notes associated with being informed.

OUT FRONT AND ALONE

We often think we're better to get out in front of an issue and talk about it before it happens. It instinctively feels honest and courageous. We often apply this approach to issues with a long history, or those that have been much publicized or talked about internally or externally. We're making a judgment call based on our thinking it's important. So, we're saying it's important. Yet it may not have been – but by our action, it is now.

It's often best not to be too hasty, to include it in the balanced mix and have our colleagues let us know what's important. In this way we avoid too defensive a posture or unbalancing our approach by inflating the importance of an issue too soon.

OUTSIDE THE RING

Change doesn't only take place within the organization. If only it were that contained.

We looked at context and environment in Part One. We'll be facing stakeholders externally as well as internally. There will be clients, customers, subscribers, vested interests and the inquisitive uninvited. For each there will be existing and new. It's highly likely that the change we're leading will need to be conveyed externally. Whether we'll need to get those affected (or likely to be by the changed state) emotionally engaged and actively involved will need to be determined at the planning stage. It may be no more than a change of phone number or email address, in which case we may have that covered.

We need to draw on the insight developed in the map we made of the external environment in which we're operating. We have a starting checklist. We can consider each of the actors against the three groups of change – information, engagement, involvement – in terms of need and method. Reconnaissance, as we said, is seldom wasted.

THE ENTERPRISE SOCIAL NETWORK

A change communication medium worth evaluating a little more is the enterprise social network (ESN). An ESN is essentially a cloud-based social network that sits behind an organization's firewall so that it's restricted to employees and authorized persons only. Many organizations now operate them, with varying degrees of success. They're a tool for developing and supporting a community. The aim is to support connection, collaboration and knowledge-sharing within the organization that otherwise wouldn't be feasible in physical space due to either geographical spread or suboptimal design.

As with many such initiatives, taking the Professor Piehead evaluation method, they've been a partial success. Where they haven't met expectations the reasons are many, varied and interrelated. These include (but aren't exclusively) lack of trust that the environment is elementally safe, only partial use at a senior level and therefore non-acceptance as a main channel of communication, and a descent into irrelevant snippy chat and backchat. We have a misplaced expectation that such networks are intuitive and that we know how to behave and get the most out of them. That's because we're used to generally available social media platforms – the type that, once liberating and inspirational, have in the main descended into irrelevant snippy chat and backchat.

ESN are very often themselves a change initiative, an evolving work-in-progress. The hope that they'll be a major contributor to another change initiative needs careful evaluation. Experience of its use thus far needs assessing along with how it might be tweaked to support the change initiative. Our initiative might be just the one to propel the ESN into mainstream, even primary, use. Alternatively, it could provide an escalation hub for negativity and unconstructive feedback. The trolls are just as likely to lurk airside as they are landside. Either way the ESN is likely to be beneficial as long as it's use for the initiative is guided.

COMMUNICATION BREAKDOWN?

The more open a conversation we've created, the more we can calibrate our success in conveying what we intend. Yet when communication fails, leaving people uninformed – it's not seen, not read, not understood, it's misinterpreted, rejected – it's rarely the fault of the audience. It's unusual for any message to reach everyone. We usually accept what might in other fields be deemed low percentage rates as success – a survey is generally deemed a success if it achieves a 50% response rate. Yet we can still aim for far higher.

There could be any reason for the communication failing – the message itself, the medium (choice of, or technicalities) or interference from other initiatives. It's highly likely, however, to be one or more of what we said, how we said it, where we said it or when. Sometimes, of course, it may be a combination of factors, or there may be no particular fathomable reason.

The inclusion in our communication strategy therefore of testing its success is vital. If we don't know that our communication has failed, then we'll have reverted to hopeful broadcast. Open rates and click-through measures are useful indicators, but they don't signify attention or understanding unless something discernible is asked for in response.

However closely we have followed the recommendations covered, we can build in some accessible fail-safes. There is none better than repetition. It doesn't have to be immediate, sometimes looping ahead one or two iterations. It could be that every new item contains a refresh of the last. The reminder "as we said last time" with a direct link can often prompt a look back at what preceded it should it have been missed or forgotten. Alternatively, including a summary of what was said last time is helpful. Repetition doesn't have to be direct. It presents an opportunity to rephrase something that may have been open to misinterpretation – we may, for instance, have become aware of a particular unintended reaction. Consider almost every television drama that airs a show weekly and begins with "Previously on ..." With the passing of time between episodes and the myriad of draws upon our attention, we'd often be lost without it.

With all of that, I'm informed. I'm just not *feeling* it yet.

I'M ENGAGED

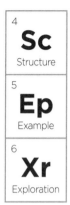

We've got the why, how, what, who, when, where, what happens next and what happens if what's supposed to happen doesn't happen (or something else happens instead) of our change initiative. We're now adding an emotional dimension. It may be that some of our communication has already created an emotional response, but that's not the whole picture and we can't rely on it entirely. Now we're going to try to actually prompt and sustain it.

There are those areas in which we can engage that are tangible: the structure we create comprising people, resources, activities and events. Then there are those in which we're engaged personally, related to the example we set through our commitments and behaviours. Finally, there are those that we participate in and experience with our colleagues, in which we can share perspectives through experimentation.

When our colleagues are engaged with the initiative, they're likely to want to know more, ask more questions and get involved. As the second group of elements, it bridges, binds and enlivens the others flanking it.

ELEMENT 4: STRUCTURE

The tangible stuff of change that prompts us to feel engaged are people and materials. The people are those who provide structure and connection with our colleagues, the materials provide colour, texture and depth beyond simply communicating. Much of this is needed before we even start communicating. We shouldn't kick off in a dry and bristly manner and start to enrich it as we progress, as a response; we need to be ready at the outset.

We engage two groups of people to then engage our colleagues – those associated with governance and those who act as a conduit with our colleagues, carrying and conveying information in both directions.

GOVERNANCE GROUPS

Let's face it, the term 'governance' sounds austere and limiting. It smacks of control, more setting out the things we can't do than those we can, giving rules and decrees. We instinctively associate all the figures through our lives who've stripped out the freewheeling fun, from the park keeper to our line manager.

But it's a word we're familiar with. It works both ways, as we'll see. We've acknowledged before that we can't do it all. In fact, there's some of it that's beyond our authority level entirely, and some where a broadly collective decision is essential. At the very least the window is too big for our backside to be hanging out all on its own. The structure and accountabilities will look something like Figure 27, the optional groups shown with dotted borders:

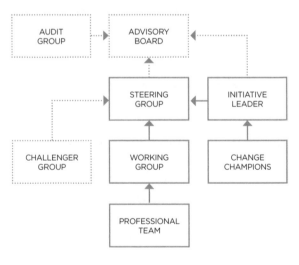

FIGURE 27

The structure we usually create is one associated with 'steering' – giving direction and keeping the initiative on track toward the vision, continuously moving. We don't steer anything that's stationary. We instantly start to decouple the negative associations. The **Steering Group** or committee (preferably the first, there's no use of committee that sounds anything but stuffy, slow and stale – a blocker) usually comprises a sponsoring executive or two, directors from functions including IT, HR, Communications, Legal and Property, and key business unit leaders. It doesn't have to be padded out with supporters and advocates either. Bringing dissenting voices into the Steering Group can be immensely valuable both for itself and the dissenters. As leaders of the initiative, we'll expect to be part of this group.

Its key functions are to set direction, release or approve expenditure, provide scrutiny to progress, inform the leaders of the initiative of changes in organizational priorities as they may affect it, and hopefully to resolve more conflict than it creates. It doesn't actually do any *work*, as such.

Someone needs to be assigned a secretarial role for ensuring agendas are set, materials are prepared, everyone shows up, records are kept and it stays interesting, or it'll quickly fall apart. If this should happen, key members will deem their absence to have deferred consent, creating confusion and rework. It's a key role, therefore.

It has to meet regularly enough to be useful but not so often as to fall victim to complacency and non-attendance. A constitution is helpful, even if half a page, so everyone knows what they're doing there. It has to have an executive mandate, or everyone sits quietly waiting for the most senior person in the room to make a decision. Its decisions must be binding on even those more senior, which means the CEO must agree that a lesser body is in this instance more powerful than they. Not always easy. We should brief the CEO beforehand, so they agree to the mandate, timescale and expenditure and so they're aware of the opportunities and risks in advance.

It should be regarded as an elementally safe environment, one able to accept and resolve challenge and differing views. That said, a Steering Group isn't a forum for throwing a member of the team under a bus. It shouldn't be used for politicking, apportioning blame, avoiding responsibility or airing grievances that could be resolved outside of the meetings. A Steering Group functioning in this manner needs resetting or reconstituting. We mustn't be afraid to do this if needed. Once created, it isn't then immune from assessment of its effectiveness. We're not Dr Frankenstein.

There are three other groups that may be convened.

Sometimes with complex initiatives or larger companies a two-tier structure is useful – a Steering Group and above it an **Advisory Board**. This is usually a more ceremonial vehicle that ensures that senior executives can be associated with the initiative by virtue of being members of a unit that meets occasionally to sanction decisions – a sort of royal assent. It gives our colleagues a clear indication that leadership are vested. Usually enough pre-briefing is achieved to make sure there are no surprises and that the meetings last no longer than a good lunch.

However well governed and intentioned, a risk always exists that an initiative might develop a degree of self-determination that sees it gradually slip outside of the organization's policies and processes in order to achieve its vision. An audit function may therefore be required. Partners or shareholders may even insist upon this. The Steering Group may perform this role, dependent upon its composition, the scale of the initiative or the degree of expenditure and commitment. Alternatively, a separate **Audit Group** may be needed comprising the appropriate functions such as Finance and Procurement to evaluate all key decisions and the process taken to arrive at them. This would likely have the most senior-level reporting line, shown here as the Advisory Board.

Where a significant change is being pursued that has longer-term impact on the organization, a **Challenger Group** comprising today's middle management and aspiring leadership is useful. These are the people who'll often be most significantly impacted and who may need to deal longer-term with the consequences of the changes. This is particularly the case in professional services firms or formal partnerships. Challenger groups need an extra spoonful of elemental safety to be empowered to speak their minds without concern, as they could potentially be questioning the decisions of both the Advisory Board *and* Steering Group.

Not essentially a governance unit but one that ensures the process works effectively is a **Working Group**. Often comprising a mix of internal and external members, it prepares decisions for the Steering Group to take, presenting options, opportunities and risks, and ensuring that the governance structure is productively employed. Ably supported and informed by the professional team (external advisors and consultants, as required), the Working Group keeps the Steering Group rightfully busy.

Any more groups and governance will start to become a self-fulfilling prophecy. We need structure, but only just enough.

CHANGE CHAMPIONS

Or 'ambassadors' (which sounds overly bureaucratic, or like an advertisement for chocolates with delusions of grandeur) or 'leads' (but that's confusing leads with leaders). These are a representative collection of advocates for the initiative drawn from the wider pool of colleagues affected. They need to be senior enough to get stuff done but not too senior that they're never available and won't prioritize the time needed. It moves a group of people into the inner circle, thereby generating involvement.

Their role is essentially as carriers of information between the colleagues they represent and the initiative leadership team, as advocates for the change, and to resolve minor local issues without them blowing up. As such, they have early access to information. As with the Steering Group, they're not always the converts either: sometimes it's good to have some committed sceptics in the mix.

They're vital. I've worked with some change champions who've literally made the difference between resounding success and stuttering mediocrity, and some we didn't know were even there at all. One I recall, with little natural authority, was like a caffeinated sheepdog, utterly committed and effective in getting his team to where they needed to be. The leadership team – and us – were massively grateful. Then, like Garibaldi after playing a major part in unifying Italy in 1861, he just went home.

The importance here is that we'd often rather hear from our colleagues than a central function or (as we may perceive) a corporate stooge. It feels much less like something is being done to us, and that we're a huge step closer to the beating heart of the initiative without having sold our soul, Faust-like, to get there.

The ratio of change champions to colleagues depends entirely on the scale and scope of the change, but the total number – as they'll need to be met with as a group – needs to be manageable. If we have to hire the Royal Albert Hall for a meeting, we've probably overdone it. It should be sized to ensure all voices can be heard. Bear in mind we have to invest in this group, taking time collectively and individually with them. They're volunteers not contracted staff, so we need to use their time effectively and respectfully, which means preparation is essential. Just as change champions can make an amazing contribution, the return on non-investment can be fatal to the initiative.

There are clear arguments for appointment being based on both volunteering and considered selection. Some people who we may want involved won't step forward, and some people who do step forward we'd rather didn't. We can manage the final selection, either way.

In terms of time invested, this can be answered in two capacities – the time we suggest they need to be able to give – say, a half day a week over the life of the initiative – and the time they actually invest because they see the need, enjoy and believe in what they're doing, and it transpires to be more interesting than the day job. We should make sure they're not *so* into the role that we get a disgruntled phone call from their manager and they're withdrawn.

CREATIVE STOCK

Our change initiative must visually come alive and be clearly and uniquely recognizable. If it looks like everything else that comes out of the sausage machine, it's going to be seen as another sausage. It therefore requires a degree of brand, even if not to the extent of a range of sportswear. Yet it's not an opportunity to get lost in creative pursuits for their own sake. It shouldn't be treated as an art-house retrospective.

We therefore need some creative stock to facilitate analogue and digital communication and engagement. Its usual components are set out in Table 9.

LOGO AND COLOUR SCHEME	Whether based on the organization's logo or palette of colours, all material will need to be recognizable as associated with the initiative.
SLIDE TEMPLATE	As much as it's in vogue to blame slide-creation software for all our corporate ills, we'll be knocking out some presentation decks. They should look fresh and compelling. And, of course, legible for 'those at the back.'
MICROSITE	A simple website within the organization's firewall as a repository for all key information, built in an accessible language and capable of being updated by the leadership team. The microsite is a home for our developing Q&A.
MICROSITE CONTENT	In addition to the expected static content, short interview films ('vox pops' – from *vox populi*, voice of the people, but not in the way a modern demagogue would summon it), demos and walkthroughs. Effectively shot content can make a huge difference.
EXHIBITION TEMPLATE	See the subsection 'Roadshows, town halls and exhibitions' in Element 6 – we'll be creating analogue display panels telling the story of the initiative in all its detail.
EMAIL BULLETIN	A regular update template that makes it stand out from the daily bombardment. News items should link to the microsite for the full story.
DAY ONE GUIDE OR MANUAL	We'll have changed things – and will need to tell everyone how it works even though we're convinced we've told them already. In addition, there will be people new to the organization who won't have been through the programme with us. They'll have no history of the change. We often assume that those arriving later won't need an explanation of how things work and why. They will.
MERCHANDISE	We'll likely have a need to recourse to the odd dash of novelty to land a point. Whether it's T-shirts, mugs or stickers – or something far more creative and appropriate – we can't underestimate the value of a sparingly deployed freebie, the more useful the better.

TABLE 9

Creative stock doesn't get knocked up on a slide deck in a lunch break. At least it shouldn't do. It's an investment. That's a posh way of saying it's going to cost money. Very often, more than any initial overall budget assumes, if it's even been thought of at all. We can do it ourselves if we have the skills and time, both of which are rare, or we'll need to commission it. Whichever way, we must be ready. It takes far longer than we ever estimate at the outset, so we need to start it straight away. There's no penalty for having the creative stock ready early.

We should also note that sometimes this investment does its job quickly and effectively. We should resist the temptation to overuse our material simply because we've paid for it. On a project I led, as the change being created was significant, the team made a short, animated film at comparatively eye-watering expense. It landed extremely well. It played to miniscule attention spans and a growing shift in importance at the organization from written to filmic communication. We had initially justified the cost based on believing we'd use it for all related future initiatives. By the time of the second major project, however, so established were the ideas from the first, that the animation wasn't used. Costly as it had been, it had thoroughly served its purpose.

If we're ever in doubt about the value of creative stock, as we covered in Element 1, we should remember how far the smiley face of the State Mutual Life Assurance Company of Massachusetts travelled. And is still travelling.

ELEMENT 5: EXAMPLE

Whenever we were about to take on something significant, a former colleague of mine from Sydney would look at me with a deadpan, serious and wistfully regretful face, shake his head and say: "Change is great, *just not for me.*"

With a change initiative there are things we do for the benefit of both ourselves and those directly affected. Our relationship with ourselves is as important as with others – if we can't be honest with, and respectful of, ourselves, then it'll directly impact how we are with others. They'll see right through our mask of sincerity, and think: "If *they* can't adapt when leading this thing, then why should we?" Our role isn't just as leaders but as standard bearers.

PERSONAL COMMITMENTS

We bridge engagement and involvement with the making of personal commitments. They help us to influence and inspire others to do things differently. They're promises to ourselves that we commit to uphold even in the face of urgent and exceptional challenges, and that we tell our colleagues about and ask them to hold us to. And we'll all do this.

These commitments are both good for us, as we test our understanding and resolve against the aims of the initiative, and beneficial in terms of the influence they have on others.

First, we make them. We identify things we can do that will create a visibility of the change. This isn't about targets or 'stretch goals' or macho demonstrations of a capacity to handle uncertainty. It's not about competition or gaming either, but about what we know we can do. There should be no risk of breaking them when subject to the slightest tweak in stress levels. They should also not be absolutes – "I'll *never* reprimand any member of my team in front of other colleagues." Words like 'never' and 'always' bind us unreasonably. We're human, we have to be fair to ourselves.

We then encourage everyone to make personal commitments by sharing ours. It's not just about us but starts with us. We set the tone and the shape of what we're committing to. It's a step toward building even stronger elemental safety, as we're creating a point of personal vulnerability.

Finally, we 'contract' with our colleagues to ensure we don't veer off track – we all agree to be bound. Agreements of this nature are made with reason and broken with emotion: deadlines, conflicting priorities, personal matters. Being held to account at this time can be incendiary, even though the pact was made willingly. "I know I told you to make sure I should always try to do this, but not right now because [insert excuse]!" We should avoid nosediving into the emotional turmoil in which a commitment is broken and bring it back to the rational place it was made, at a less-charged time when the discussion can be had calmly. "I'm not sure if you're aware, but yesterday when it was all kicking off you reprimanded Steve in front of everyone. You'd committed not to. Is there anything we can do to help?" Once again, the power of a question.

SETTING AN EXAMPLE

Personal commitments are a natural segue into outward, demonstrable behaviour change. They're a key aspect of influence that we covered in Part One.

As leaders we set an example through what we do (our acts) and don't do (our omissions). Whether we like it or not, we give or deny permission. This percolates as far as the organizational pyramid flattens, until it reaches the baseline. Leadership behaviour is a key creator of culture, whether good, bad or ugly.

Our primitive herding instinct means we're still highly likely to copy behaviour rather than form our own judgment. Or at least before forming it. As the polymath Albert Schweitzer said, "Example is not the main thing in influencing others, it is the *only* thing."[101] Similarly, the American moral and social philosopher Eric Hoffer remarked, "When people are free to do as they please, they usually imitate others."[102] That is, even when we *could* do something else, we still copy.

The marketing guru Robert Cialdini created six principles of influence[103] that he believed would help persuade others: reciprocity, consistency, social proof, liking, authority and scarcity. In this regard, the one that stands out is consistency – making our word public, and then actively and visibly sticking to it. The visible aspect is important. Our example can't be consistent if no one is aware of it.

Another of Cialdini's principles, social proof – copying others because it feels like the right or appropriate thing to do, often in situations of uncertainty – is also a form of nudge, covered earlier in this chapter. The example we set, creating social proof, may well steer others toward a desirable behaviour in this regard.

In one initiative in which I was involved, in a bid to give colleagues greater freedom of when, where and how to work, we encouraged leaders who were members of the organization's gym to visit at varying times of the day. Our colleagues weren't responding simply by us saying it was okay to do so. One afternoon a Director slung his kit bag over his shoulder and announced to his team he was off to work out, immediately following it up with the ruinous, "I'm not skiving!" When we set an example, we have to do so with full confidence even if somewhere inside we're fighting demons. Otherwise we simply reinforce the entrenched behaviour we're trying to liberate. That day the CFO did go to the gym in the middle of the afternoon and was seen doing so. For all those who didn't hear his comment it was noted – if it's okay for him, it's okay for us. Mid-afternoon gym attendance rose.

One of the most under-expressed yet over-felt criticisms of change is that – like the future – it's unevenly distributed. The worst outcome of all is the *Animal Farm*-esque inequality that results from leaders either (or both) considering themselves, or acting as if, out of scope of the change and therefore insulated from it. Leaders must be *behaviourally* in scope even when out of scope. Change has to be visibly all-inclusive.

Leadership behaviour defines the outer limits of organizational culture, too. In this respect omissions can sometimes be even more powerful than acts. Tolerating poor behaviour, not intervening to curtail it, signifies its acceptability. As leaders we need to be consistent, or the boundaries become uncertain. Holes in the fence are an invitation too great for some. Over time they become even more difficult to repair – if we can even find them at all.

At this juncture we can bring values (covered in Part One), stories (in Part Two) and behaviour together. It's well-trodden territory and so it's likely that a diagram similar to Figure 28 has been depicted elsewhere. The starting point could be values or behaviours. The behaviours could be acts or omissions. It shows how the values of the organization might progressively strengthen through behaviours and stories. It could also work negatively, however, with stories being told of poor behaviour serving to undermine values.

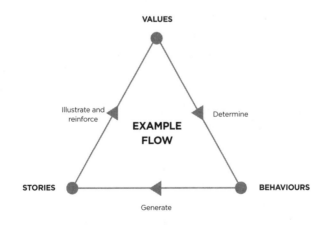

FIGURE 28

It's not just leaders who can influence behaviour, however; it's all of us. Hoffer's comment on imitating others wasn't just directed at those in the top floor corner office. Or those of us leading a change initiative.

Erica Chenoweth, a political scientist at Harvard University, noted through extensive research into political activism and non-violent protest that it only takes around 3.5% of the population actively participating to ensure serious political change.[104] It's not necessarily all about leadership, it's about influence. Dissent can be a conscious and explicit rejection of leadership behaviour. Often leaders have less influence than they think and those being led have more. That said, it certainly doesn't let leaders off the hook.

DOING THINGS DIFFERENTLY

We covered the theoretical basis of adoption and adaptation in Part One with a distinct preference for strategies based on the latter. We can either tell people everything they need to do (wholly adoption led – a push strategy) or have them work out what opportunities exist and find their own way (entirely adaptation led – a pull strategy).

With the 'low risk, low reward' adoption route we provide information, instruction and expectations. We inform people of how to master the new tasks. You used to do x, now you need to do y. "This is the difference between x and y. This is how you do y." It doesn't necessitate an account of whether leaving x to do y is either desirable or practicable, it's simply a requirement. There will be notes to take away.

The adaptation method is firmly rooted in engagement – with higher risk, higher reward. It's about shaping behavioural change, not just creating a new routine. We first provide a full description of the new situation or scenario, including why it's being created, how it'll work and what'll be different. Yet instead of instructing, we facilitate discussion and planning among those affected to determine how best to use the opportunities presented to do things differently. It takes the form "We're doing *x*, how do we think we can get to *y* in order to [outcome and benefit]?"

In this sense it's guided learning. The key difference is that in being subject to the change initiative, we're invested – not just as individuals, but as a team. We're not *following* rules given to us, we're using the resources available to *make* the rules together. As leaders we're in the room with our colleagues, helping frame the outcome, but not dictating it.

We therefore have to be among the earliest to start doing things differently, and we have to 'work out loud.'[105] This means talking about why we're doing it in a new way and what it entails. We can't rely on being observed only. We have to take the change to our colleagues. Working out loud means doing things differently amongst them.

We'll see more of this in the next chapter as engagement turns to activity (Element 8).

ELEMENT 6: EXPLORATION

Having explored a host of individual things we can do, with an initiative of any scale we'll need to create some mass engagement. There can be more personal threads to these events, but they're generally intended to reach as many people as possible. The space between events shouldn't be filled with anxiety-bubbling silence. We need to ensure there's a feedback loop. They're interventions in a connected, active timeline, not islands.

ROADSHOWS, TOWN HALLS AND EXHIBITIONS
There are three broad types of event (set out in Table 10), all of which involve taking the information and resources to those affected by the change.

TYPE	WHAT	FOR	AGAINST
ROADSHOWS 1: many	A high-level presentation on what's about to happen, why, how and when	Can reach a lot of people quickly Can be held online as well as in person Anyone can/ should attend – no participation needed Opportunity for high-level introduction before anything begins Can cover a lot of ground quickly	High-level, little specific detail Feels one-way – broadcast Only useful occasionally – not a substitute for communication The initiative team learn very little
TOWN HALLS 1: many	A presentation on progress with open Q&A with leaders	Provides a feedback opportunity Can be held online as well as in person Can show the human side of an initiative with leaders held publicly to account Questions allow any issue or concern to be raised – even difficult ones	Discourages introverts from participating Can allow extroverts to monopolize the event Can surface emotion and negativity that becomes infectious Requires experienced facilitators
EXHIBITIONS 1:1	A full and detailed explanation of progress to date arranged on multiple boards, facilitated by many of the team	Comfortingly analogue and tactile – creates a relaxed environment Allows attendees to stay as long as they want Inclusive Many aspects of expertise available Learning opportunity for the initiative team	Time-consuming Expensive to produce and arrange Important issues may get lost in the intimacy, rolled up and aggregated

TABLE 10

With any such events, we need to watch out for even the slightest signs of self-congratulatory tone or behaviour. High-fives and backslapping are evidence that perhaps they're on the wrong track. The aim of each, despite their respective pros and cons, is a blend of disclosure and critique.

All are useful as long as they're all deployed at some point but not overused. It's not a case of: "Here are three methods, pick one." All roadshows, and our colleagues could be forgiven for thinking the change is never going to happen. All town halls, and they may think we're stoking a revolution, and are about to proclaim a new republic. All exhibitions, and they may become overwhelmed by granularity and potentially miss the bigger issues and concerns that may allow us the time to do something about them. It could beneficially run something like Figure 29, with the spaces between comprising continuing dialogue.

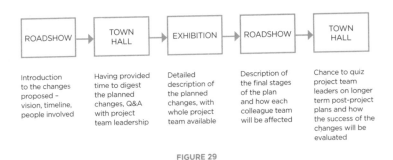

FIGURE 29

Vital with all three is a clear and discernible response where matters are raised by our colleagues: a playback that reflects the event has taken place, what was raised, what has been (and will be) done about it and what happens next. This includes why something might not be done, too, as the events aren't an open exercise in order taking. Any small requests that are actionable immediately should be both done and confirmed as done. It reinforces the fact that dialogue is two-way, continuous and worthwhile, and that it has an outcome.

EXPERIMENTS AND PILOTS

Experiments and pilots follow from roadshows, town halls and exhibitions, in which we were just talking about it. Now we're doing some of it, too. The exploration becomes tangible.

'Experiment' and 'pilot' are often used interchangeably. We deploy both in a change initiative where we have the time. In either instance we're putting something to our colleagues to test what we're thinking or have done to date and providing the opportunity for feedback that may help refine or alter our approach. They provide tangibility, access, and a visible dimension to the initiative. Everyone should know what was hypothesized, proven or unsuccessful, and what happens next. They're opportunities for co-creation with the recipients of the change.

While both are incredibly useful change tools, they're substantially different in several respects, as laid out in Table 11.

	EXPERIMENT	PILOT
TIMING	It's an early-stage test of a hypothesis or idea, usually with a hunch that it may work or that something may emerge from which learning can be gleaned. Think test tubes and chemicals, loud noises, the odd "Eureka!" but often an inconclusive result with a need for more work or thought. Or both.	It comes later. It's a manifestation of the developed idea, almost the finished article with a few edges still to file down. It may be the fine-tuning of an earlier experiment, in which far more is now known and in which the glitches have been all but ironed out.
SCOPE	We're specific. We've pinpointed something we want to test. It should be small scale. Too wide and we'll learn nothing. There must be a degree of control given the other loose players involved. Establishing cause is important so we can't afford to lose it in the noise.	We can be general in our scope as our control over everything in play is tight, the experimentation was over some time ago. We'll aim to learn about a wide range of small things.
EXPECTATION	The idea is to learn, and that could be as open-ended as we like. Testing, measurement and feedback will be vital components. We may have also reconciled ourselves to the idea of failure in part or whole. We're early enough that it doesn't matter. Too much.	The idea is to validate. We're hopeful of almost complete success. We know what we expect to see. We're also testing the success of our change strategy to date – if there's confusion, we may have missed something. Or a lot. We're aiming for refinement, not enlightenment.
LEARNING	We expect to learn a lot, with distinct signposts to future study or work. If we don't learn much from our experiment, it's likely we didn't push the boundaries enough, we didn't set it up properly or the feedback channel wasn't open or clear enough.	We expect to gain detailed but vital insights. If we're learning huge amounts from a pilot, we've probably created an experiment and are therefore under some pressure against our schedule as we'll be redesigning and reworking as a result.

TABLE 11

KEEPING PROGRESS VISIBLE

Demonstrating that the initiative has both started and is progressing is vital. Yet 'quick wins' may just be the 'lowest-hanging fruit' of corporate cliché. They satisfy our need for immediate transactional return. Those involved can point to attributable achievement. Every change initiative wants them, however urgent. They're the fast food of organizational life, pumped full of sawdust, rusk and fluid, immediate yet ultimately unsatisfying. We get quite hooked on them for this very reason. They may be just as bad for us.

There are arguments in the existing literature that use quick wins (or other expressions for them such as 'results-seeking projects') in support of an earlier assertion in the book that we're all change professionals first, and that all leadership and management roles are change roles. Robert Schaffer, for example, contends that making managers responsible for a host of such smaller projects with results that can be assured reinforces this mindset and behaviour.[106] I'm not entirely sure what projects that are *not* intended to produce results might be termed.

However, there are four key considerations. First, if they were that obvious, why hadn't they been done already? They can be an admission of past neglect or disinterest. Second, we need to be careful that quick wins aren't seen *as* the initiative, and that after one or two completed tasks the energy dissipates, and everyone thinks it's over. At this stage the enthusiasm for the tougher stages may wane. Third, they can pump a collective ego full of hot air, believing its own hype. In this respect they can make a team less prepared for what is to come. Finally, we need to show the unexpected to maintain interest and energy. We rather love surprises – we mentioned their contribution to the art of storytelling in Part Two.

Rather than quick wins, it's better, instead, to think of *visible signs of progress*, balanced between the easy and the not-so-easy. We'll get even progress, not a splurge of movement followed by a juddering halt as it all gets trickier. We should be prepared to take on some tough stuff early. It shows courage and ambition. It also tests the team's resolve and skill. We can open a dialogue with those impacted and generate feedback. We won't learn much from simply doing what should have been done a long time ago.

TROJAN MICE

Visible progress can also be achieved using a technique that has been termed 'Trojan mice.' It's an idea of Peter Fryer brought to my attention by Euan Semple, author of *Organizations Don't Tweet, People Do*. Euan describes them as "small, well focused changes, which are introduced on an ongoing basis in an inconspicuous way. They're small enough to be understood and owned by all concerned but their effects can be far-reaching."[107]

Instead of waiting for us all to build the wooden horse, drawing in huge amounts of time, people, money, planning and management, we can set ideas running that start the process of change – and just as importantly an *openness to* change – much earlier. Dave Snowden (to whom we referred earlier as the creator of the Cynefin framework) calls them 'safe-to-fail probes' that allow us to test the context in which we're operating.[108] The approach is aligned with the Agile methodology covered in Part Two.

Clearly, once released, mice are hard to control and tend to multiply with staggering commitment. Yet that's rather the point. Thinking about our operating system, an elementally safe environment makes the mice all the more effective and motivated once released. Where there is no safety, the traps are often set. If we recall our focus on the opportunity in Part Two, Figure 15 now starts to look like Figure 30.

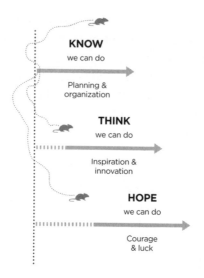

FIGURE 30

The effectiveness of Trojan mice is echoed by Khurshed Dehnugara and Claire Genkai Breeze in the assertion that "there is a paradox at the heart of significant ambitions – they're best realized through small beginnings."[109] It's a change of emphasis and language from the bullish corporate 'win,' imbued as it is with struggle, resistance mitigation and force to a far more exploratory and inquisitive approach likely to generate interaction and learning. It feels like mountain air.

We do, however, have to avoid the somewhat in-vogue temptation to lurch straight to the opposite – forget x, it's now all about y. That is, from large-scale corporate change – the Trojan horse – to a marshalled fleet of safe-to-fail Trojan mice. The success lies in the balance: vision with enough structure and organization aligned with a preparedness to release and test small ideas, to experiment. An initiative that's all Trojan mice would be chaos. It's about xy.

I'M ENGAGED: OR AM I?

We have our governance structures and change resources in place, personal commitments made, and exploration planned. We're taking the change initiative to our colleagues in practical and interesting ways. Yet there are some cautionary notes associated with being engaged.

MEANING IT

If we wish to engage people, they have to know we mean it. To paraphrase Hemingway from Part Two, the best way for them to know we mean it is to mean it. Therefore, if we have any residual doubt, we have to deal with it. Either by accepting that there's something still to discover or learn and so we'll keep an open mind, or investing more time in seeking clarification and reassurance. If it's even vaguely apparent that we don't mean it, that we're just going through the motions, we'll be found out. We dress our beliefs in the complex array of words and actions we deploy. I once interviewed a very well-qualified and experienced change leader for a project role, who didn't appear to be entirely convinced by the underlying philosophy of the initiative. He knew how to run a project. Yet there was just something about his approach, manner, expression. I'm not even sure I knew what at the time. It was deflating. When challenged, he confessed that he harboured doubts. As a result, we didn't take it any further, which was probably best for both of us.

FEELING IT

There's communication within engagement and there are clear links and relationships between the two. Yet engagement is different, and as vital. If we want our colleagues to feel it, we have to put feeling *into* it. That means emphasis, colour, zest, life, three dimensions instead of two. It may not compare with seeing our team hit a last-minute cup final winner or having our favourite guitarist sign our forearm with a permanent marker, but it has to *register*.

GOING OVERBOARD

And then there's feeling it a little too much. That is, not allowing us to register an emotional response in our own space and time but rather forcing it on us – "You *will* get excited about this initiative!" This is why our work on lexicon and tone was essential. It keeps us in check and prevents a rapid descent into a festival of frivolity that eventually turns everyone away. We've probably been at those meetings where the grasp on reality gets abandoned faster than inhibitions at a tequila tasting. It's engagement, not engagement at all costs, that we're aiming for. We have to be as prepared to rein in the enthusiasm as much as we're prepared to ramp it up. We own the balance.

THE ANXIETY ENGINE

Anxiety is a nervousness, worry or unease about something happening or that's about to happen. As in, to all intents and purposes, a change initiative. It's often mentioned in the same breath as stress and considered to be a milder version. However, the difference is more related to time. Stress is a shorter-term response to a particular threat, while anxiety is more likely to be chronic. It's not just a response to things we don't like or think we may not. We can just as readily experience it related to things about to happen that we're looking forward to and are excited about. It can be debilitating and damaging physiologically and emotionally. We can start to experience anxiety from the moment communication begins – before, if we've heard the whispers on the corporate wires. But at the point where we seek emotional engagement, anxiety begins to ramp up for our colleagues.

Yet we're not asking everyone to blindly embrace the unequivocally optimistic philosophy of Professor Pangloss from Voltaire's *Candide*: "All is for the best in the best of all possible worlds."[110] We need to be open to the anxiety that will arise and do all we can to turn it to a positive mindset. We can't dismiss it in annoyance or submit to it and accommodate every request or exception. We do have to maintain an openness to listening and responding. Within the more personally expressed and less rationally articulated offerings may well lurk useful insight, we just need to look and listen a little harder to reveal it. In short, we need to work with anxiety as it ebbs and flows, not against it.

THE FORLORN HOPE

Trojan mice and exploratory safe-to-fail initiatives are to be encouraged, but leaving them exposed can also be counter-productive. Broader culture-change initiatives will comprise many aspects, each of which on its own may help begin the process, give it momentum – or get blasted.

'Forlorn hope' was the name, commonly used in the English Civil Wars (1642-51), for those soldiers sent into a breach in the walls of a defended fortification where the risk of casualties was extremely high. We can condemn our initiatives to this fate if we're not careful. We might confidently convince ourselves of the viability, common sense or safety of an idea and turn the attempt to create visible progress into visible embarrassment. It can knock our credibility in the process.

At one time, faced with attempting to move an organization to a position of championing personal health and wellbeing in line with its external brand positioning, my team decided to review the food and drink offer in the corporate headquarters cafeteria where no charge was made for lunch. Despite the fact that the new menu was far fresher and healthier and therefore represented the sensible choice, with clear information about calories, salt, fat and other goodies, it was roundly rejected. As an initiative it was far too isolated. As an emotional matter, it needed the protection of being included within a multifaceted, broad cultural shift, one among many varying-sized initiatives. It required a time-consuming retreat and reset to become accepted. It was eventually, in a slightly modified form.

With all of that, I'm informed and engaged. I'm just not *involved* yet.

I'M INVOLVED

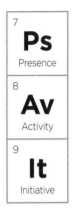

While we may be fully informed and highly engaged, we may or may not be involved.

Being involved in this regard means partaking in activity specifically geared toward a successful outcome. Unlike being informed and engaged, it involves a particular time or energy commitment. It means consciously deciding to do *this* rather than doing something else. It's evidently easier to get people involved when they know what's going on and why. It's a rare type who's happy to get involved but couldn't give two hoots about the context of what they're doing.

Engagement creates a temporary bond, more a letter of intent – involvement cements this into a form of social contract. As such, generating the involvement of our colleagues requires time, effort and commitment on our part, but invariably returns on the investment.

Involvement has long been regarded as vital to the attaining of wisdom. The Chinese philosopher Xun Kuang, known as Xunzi (310-235 BCE), in a quote attributed to many others, stated that: "Not hearing is not as good as hearing, hearing is not as good as seeing, seeing is not as good as knowing, knowing is not as good as acting; true learning continues until it is put into action." [111]

Yet it's the power of each in (dare I say it?) synergy that's most effective in creating and leading change. While it follows that the more informed and engaged we are the more likely we are to get involved, it doesn't mean we wait to communicate and engage before organizing anything likely to generate involvement. We get on with it.

WHY GET INVOLVED?

When our colleagues show up, there will be a host of reasons why. They include one or more of the following in each case.

Beneficial reasons:
- It's interesting
- It feels worthwhile
- I feel I can make a difference
- It's the right thing to do
- I recognize that I have skills or experience that the initiative needs
- I may learn something

Beneficial **enough** reasons:
- It makes me feel needed
- I feel I ought to as my colleagues are
- I've been asked to
- I may get something out of it
- It'll benefit my career prospects
- I'll be 'in the know'
- I don't want it to later emerge that I wasn't involved

Reasons we'd **rather not** be entertaining:
- I've been told to
- I've got nothing else to do
- I don't like what I'm doing so I'll do this instead
- It seems like an opportunity to make trouble
- I want it to fail

Clearly, we're targeting motivations from the first group as far as we're able. However, once involved, where the driver is from the second or third group, we have the opportunity to shift their perspective to the most beneficial type. When our colleagues aren't involved, it's more likely to solidify their negativity. We need to bring our colleagues in.

CHARACTERISTICS OF INVOLVEMENT

All involvement isn't the same. Unlike the preceding two groups of elements of change, with involvement we need to set out some specific characteristics.

First, there's a distinction to be made between **feeling** and **being** involved. We may be supportive of the change, see and sense the involvement of others and be appreciative, just not actually *do* anything of note our self. Yet when quizzed on our sense of involvement we'd wholly agree that we were. Feeling involved may be anything from active association (flag-waving, real or virtual), making personal commitments to change (whether shared or not), or helping colleagues where uncertainty may exist (whether invited to do so or not). It's a small step on from engagement.

It may for us simply be a less-than-academic interpretation of terminology, where we claim to feel involved but wouldn't naturally use the term 'engaged.' Being realistic, while we've used it here and we do so in the workplace, whoever uses it at home? How many times have we felt 'engaged' in the pub at the prospect of Scruttock's Old Dirigible making a guest-ale appearance? We can *feel* involved without actually lifting a finger. *Being* involved, on the other hand, means actually *doing* something. Our aim is to achieve both with as many of our colleagues as possible.

Second, as alluded to in the drivers, is the question of whether the involvement is **compulsory** or **voluntary**. If compulsory, we're likely to be clearer on what we need to do and why, yet less enthusiastic about doing it (unless it helpfully means we have to do less of something else or there is a tangible reward at the end). Trying to extricate ourselves doesn't always play out. I once worked in Germany with a manager who'd been instructed to learn Six Sigma in order to become part of a multinational project team he was keen to avoid, and so was looking for a valid reason to decline.

He claimed he couldn't do so due to his business English being weak. He was subsequently co-opted onto the team, drafted onto the Six Sigma course *and* sent for extra English lessons.

While it may be helpful to cajole our colleagues into becoming involved in an aspect of the initiative, particularly where we know a benefit may accrue, we're aiming for voluntary involvement. Our target is that our colleagues are sufficiently informed and engaged to want to take the next (literal) step.

Third, we need to respect that the **capacity** to become involved may vary. We'll have to both *be* somewhere else and *do* something else and not everyone can, all of the time. Involvement is rarely instead of the day job, it's usually in addition to. Capacity limitations will be both genuine (I really can't) and inflated (I really don't want to). Unwilling and disgruntled involvement won't benefit anyone. Those with teenage children will empathize.

Finally, there's the matter of the **quality** of involvement. This isn't necessarily proportional to time. A few minutes of inspired idea-generation or interaction could outstrip weeks of footslogging. I once worked on a property transaction in Austria where, it having become bogged down in detail, a colleague of the broker representing our team realized he'd been at school with the landlord and so offered to help. In a half-hour meeting he secured a super deal for ourselves and received the full commission, much to the chagrin of our organization's CFO who was all for settling on an hourly rate. We never know what may transpire with those involved, but we'll probably have an idea of the outcomes we'd like to see. A little targeting doesn't go amiss.

In managing each of these characteristics of involvement, while we can't guarantee a valuable outcome for our colleagues and the initiative, we can certainly do our best to set it up.

ELEMENT 7: PRESENCE

For our colleagues, the first stride to active involvement is simply being there. We covered in Element 6 a series of events including road-shows, town halls, exhibitions, experiments and pilots. Other opportunities we can offer in this regard include the following:

- Surgeries: where members of the initiative team are available to answer questions of any nature from those impacted by the change;
- Lunch-and-learn sessions: where specific aspects of the initiative are discussed in an informal and open environment; and
- Our own attendance, as leaders of the initiative, at the meetings and events of our colleagues, where we are given a slot amongst the regular business of the teams concerned.

At each we need to do everything possible to encourage attendance. Not only is a full room important, but we set the pattern. Empty seats and tumbleweed suggest this isn't worthwhile so don't bother in the future. We don't seem to forget the wide-open spaces. Time may be a friend in respect to ensuring everything gets done but is often problematic when it comes to maintaining interest amongst those affected. Attendance usually declines with time unless the stories told convey that it's worthwhile.

We'll explore the meaningful steps we can take to encourage and build involvement. I've based these on the activist Lisa Fithian's work[112] in this regard. As change leaders within organizations, we can learn a lot from social movements, at the heart of which is involvement. I've edited Fithian's eight steps down to six. We'll cover the first two steps in this section and the remaining four in the next.

Step 1: Request involvement. In seeking to get our colleagues involved, it can be especially powerful if it's a personal invitation. While it may require a lot more work, if it appears to be addressed to us personally rather than a general "Who wants to do *x*?" distribution, we're more likely to respond positively. When we ask it's rare that there are no takers at all. A proportion of people will have time on their hands, want the inside track, want to feel valued or want to be *seen* to be involved.

If it's still a struggle, we can incentivize. The threshold for a ROI is often very low. I've seen people go to great lengths for a free espresso shot. Consider how many times we respond to surveys to be included in a prize draw about which there's little information on our chances, or when it'll be made. We perform a fleeting calculation that a few minutes of pressing buttons may return the latest tablet computer and we think it's worth the investment. So, it doesn't even need to offer a guaranteed return, however small, to be effective.

As a general rule, therefore, we have to make it interesting or vital enough. We can't create contagious momentum if we haven't got anything that's worth catching. We should make it interesting in that we just want to know, or (preferably *and*) vital in that we feel we ought or need to know, as it affects us. It might be hard to whip up frenzied mass enthusiasm about a change in tax regulations but if we work on tax regulation, we'll know that understanding the changes is essential or we'll be heading for irrelevance.

Part of the interest we create may be in *not* disclosing everything at the point of invitation, generating enough curiosity to ensure presence. Being intrigued is quite a motivation. It's straight out of film marketing – the drip feed, increasingly dramatic tranches of plot and scene. We don't go straight from zero to *Brodie's Notes* via video. There's often a brain-hijacking question, which takes us back to Part One. "How far would you go to … [insert plot line]?" We can't help it; we start thinking about how far we'd go. If it turns out not to be far, we even feel guilty.

With our tumbleweed-mitigating request to be there, we're casting the net widely. We want as many people as possible to hear and see the information and have a chance to ask questions. But as we start to focus on more active involvement, the desire to simply achieve volume leads us to seek meaningful participation. That means the right people all doing more.

Step 2: Include everyone. We shouldn't always invite just the enthusiasts and supporters, however tempting this may be. We've touched on this at several junctures in the book so far. It's often better to have those who doubt the change initiative on the inside, where they can ask questions and learn more than they might when on the outside. If we exclude the sceptics and objectors, we'll only reinforce their suspicion that it's happening regardless and strengthen their opposition. It sends a signal too, informing other colleagues that those who've voiced objection – and may still continue to do so – now wear the team colours. I'm a great believer that even in the most flagrantly wilful opposition there are threads of insight. We need to bring it in.

ELEMENT 8: ACTIVITY

In order for our colleagues to get involved *actively*, as a minimum they have to know that something good or worthwhile will come of it, whether that be for the initiative or themselves. In this case it's not just the level of interest or its vital nature.

We do have to bear in mind that our goal will never be 100% involvement. Even what might be termed 'mass' participation will still only be a healthy percentage. Consider what level is regarded positively when it comes to electoral turnout or survey responses (as we touched on earlier in Part Three). The scale of those who don't participate when given a chance to influence the outcome in exchange for minimal effort is always puzzling.

We must make sure our aims are proportionate to the request, but as with buy in (covered in Part Two, in the chapter 'Cautionary tales'), this isn't a popularity contest.

We continue our six steps.

Step 3: Set expectations. We need to make it clear what it is we expect our colleagues to do. If we're asking them to give of their time, we have to be very specific. We're not just going through the motions, nor inviting them in for a comfortable chat. We therefore have to make it evident what will result, or at least what we hope will. It also ties in with Step 4 as we'll cover later – start small and build. We need to make the initial tasks manageable.

Some of the specific activities at this stage may relate to any of the following. Of particular relevance are activities at the front and back end of an initiative as the bulky middle usually involves a degree of more specialist activity:

- Experiences: story capture related to day-to-day experiences in the area affected – what works, what doesn't work and what might be better (often called 'keep/ditch/create' or similar). The power of three once again.
- Briefing: either in general or related to specific subtopics. Design often involves specialisms and adheres to a tight programme but capturing briefing information at the outset and reviewing it at periodic junctures enables constructive involvement. It tees up the 'you told us/we did' playback, vital to relate the changes taking place to the needs of those affected. It often minimizes the involvement of consultants other than to facilitate, avoiding the charge of the organization doing what it wants regardless.
- Specific fixes: intensive workshops to try to resolve specific blockers or challenges, often to processes involving multiple teams and interfaces.
- Integrations: where silos or separate functions are required to work together or to potentially combine as part of the change initiative.

In each instance a clearly defined scope and outcome framework can draw in a tranche of advocates through association.

Step 4: Prompt enquiry. During these activities we need to encourage people to ask questions – of us and each other. Active involvement shouldn't be a one-way flow, or as leaders of the change we won't learn anything or gather any insight. Involvement should be energized, analytical and critical. It should look, feel and operate like a network, not a hub and spokes. We won't know everything and so we're constantly testing and checking by invitation. There will be times where we can learn from our colleagues engaging with one another. We're not inviting involvement to have our ego massaged, we're seeking to ensure a better outcome.

Step 5: Provide context. We need to show clearly how each task we're asking our colleagues to undertake fits in with the rest. Everyone involved should know how the work of others is dependent on them, to the extent that it may even make people's lives better – working lives, at least. This shouldn't be overstated, though. We needn't inflate every mission to celestial status, we still need to be realistic. Yet activities such as these may have deep and broad implications for the initiative.

Step 6: Maintain accountability. Where our colleagues have become involved, we need to ensure they remain accountable for the effectiveness of their contribution. Responsibility comes with the admission ticket. We need to check that the activity they've signed up to is taking place, that it's meeting the brief, that we're making collective progress. It's tricky when we've asked people to give of their time and energy to ask them to see it as needing to be productive work. But involvement in a change initiative isn't a reason to skip the day job, it's to make a positive difference. So, we need to keep in mind that we need to manage the time, performance and output of this involvement effectively.

GAMIFICATION

To drive both presence and activity, turning participation into a game creates a competitive element likely to initiate and sustain it. Gamification isn't new, but it's risen to prominence in recent years with technologies that make it much easier and simpler to organize and deliver, and the interface more appealing.

We either play against our self or others. It can consist of any amount of recognition, accolades, leader boards, ladders, points or social ranking. There are usually rules (unless it's the preposterous Eton-only Wall Game – replicating it isn't recommended) and governance, both as objective as possible. The gamified activities can generate an enthusiasm that leads to the self-organized injection of competition in other associated activities. Sometimes it's enough just to start the ball rolling, so to speak. Fear of missing out (FOMO) can draw in even the most reluctant participants.

I was initially a sceptic when it came to gamification. With one particular project the status that accumulated via obtaining stickers on a card from attending and participating in events and interventions during the programme felt twee. Yet take-up was huge, and I willingly conceded. The learning for me was never to underestimate our competitive spirit and sense of play, particularly in a corporate setting when all around us can seem unduly dry and serious.

There are downsides, of course. The competition can submerge the message and set aside the engagement that was so patiently achieved. It can become everything. Games can erode relationships through fair play or foul. We discover that some colleagues are given to winning at all costs, whatever the stakes. There naturally surfaces a temptation to cheat and generate mistrust, precisely the opposite of our intent, and once-friendly competition can work its way to malicious rivalry. The negative momentum released can be hard to rebottle. Games can be a huge distraction from other necessary activity, like the small matter of work, the dry and serious stuff we mentioned. They also have an effect on decreasing attention span due to the immediacy of the reward. Lastly, the novelty, just like that of Christmas socks, is often short-lived.

While a useful component, we need to handle gamification with caution and use it sparingly. It's not a panacea or a substitute for other thought and effort.

ELEMENT 9: INITIATIVE

From turning up to getting involved, we have one final tranche of activity – that taken willingly and without invitation or compulsion in service of the change. It can either begin with the leadership team, as in making suggestions and starting a process, or entirely outside the formal initiative. Some of our colleagues will have Trojan mice of their own.

Initiative taken by those caring enough to want to make a beneficial contribution can be an inspiring thing to see. It can also be an unmitigated disaster when well-meaning activity generates an outcome we don't want. A few Trojan mice released by our colleagues can be fascinating, but an overenthusiastic infestation can paralyse. We really don't want to end up in Hazchem suits fumigating the skirting boards. We can, in turn, guide initiative, suggesting where it may be useful or appreciated, creating the channels we need explored.

TUMMELING

The most striking example of initiative in this regard can be termed 'tummeling.' Interpretations vary slightly, but *tummel* is a Hebrew word meaning commotion. It originates from the German word *tummeln* meaning 'to stir.' As a non-English word I'm not even sure if I can add an –ing or an –er to tummel.

A tummeler in the manner in which it's commonly understood is someone at a wedding who encourages others to join in the dancing. There's comparatively little written about the subject (one of the only references I found was by someone plagiarizing my description in *The Elemental Workplace*), and it's safe to say, as an idea from the early stages of the growth of social media, that it hasn't really caught on. Undeterred, I'm convinced it still has mileage as I've seen its value.

It was introduced to me by a friend, Lloyd Davis, whose role 'Social Artist in Residence' at the now-defunct Centre for Creative Collaboration (C4CC) in London's Kings Cross was, in fact, tummeling. Lloyd learned of the term from the three founders of the *tummelvision.tv* website in the USA, Deborah Schultz, Heather Gold and Kevin Marks. The website is still live, but it's been dormant for a few years.

The C4CC was an incubator centre for new innovation, comprising small units with a few people in each, all pursuing very separate ideas and ventures. Lloyd's role was to quietly yet purposefully bring people together to explore common interests and create social and collaborative life in the building. Hence it's since been applied in some instances to the creation and curation of community at co-working centres.

For our purposes, though, tummelers aren't appointed – they're identified and encouraged to do their own thing. They'll be part of our colleague group, and we'll probably see them in action. They'll be working at the fringes to bring people in, looking for those not yet engaged or involved and guiding them toward the centre. In conversation, Lloyd described tummeling as "doing things differently and talking about doings things differently."[113] The rise to prominence of social media platforms owes much to the early tummelers. They're our unofficial, undesignated, unrecognized centrifugal force. All we need to give them is a little direction and a lot of freedom. Tummelers will stir an interest in others getting involved. We must just take care not to formalize the role, create objectives, or manage them in a traditional sense. In this regard, the six steps to getting people involved don't apply here. We should, instead, tummel the tummelers, and watch.

As with gamification, reliance on tummelers is complementary to, and not a substitute for, a more structured approach to resourcing the initiative. It's possible they'll not exist or emerge. We can't create them, but we may be able to prompt them into life. The informality can lead to lopsided influence or biased emphasis. The benefit – that there's little or no control – can also be the problem. To a huge extent, their contribution is down to luck. However, the more interesting we make the whole initiative, the more likely we are to encourage their emergence.

There's no downside to that.

I'M INVOLVED – OR AM I?

With our final three elements of change – presence, activity and initiative – we've got people on their feet, energized and committed. They show up. They do stuff when we ask them. They do stuff they think is needed even when we don't ask them. They care. Yet as with the previous two groups, informed and engaged, there are some cautionary notes. While at the beginning of the chapter we stated that we need to bring our colleagues in, we can't assume that all involvement will be constructive all of the time – we'll need to manage it.

TAKING OVER

Perhaps they care a little too much and think they could do a better leadership job than us. That's always possible, of course. They believe they have second sight. Welcome involvement turns to annoying and even disruptive interference. It can be a fine line and one we're not sure has been crossed until it's been well and truly traversed. While being driven by good and often honest intentions, the help needs to be quietly and decisively stood down. If this can't be achieved directly by ourselves, the ambitious colleagues may need to be recalled to their team for a mission of the utmost importance. Just not ours.

UNDERMINING

On some occasions, involvement can have a subversive intent. Unfortunately, we never really know who might turn out to have such an agenda. We invite our colleagues in, including those who oppose what we're trying to do. Occasionally, one or more may see a window of opportunity to destabilize or discredit the initiative. It becomes resistance. Such activity rarely starts out being conducted with headlights on full beam despite the temptation. It's more likely to be enacted in persistently underhand and unattributable ways. Over time, however, the perpetrators usually reveal themselves through over-confidence, as the desire for attention becomes insatiable. At this point we need to quietly manage them out with as little fuss as possible.

TAKING IT SERIOUSLY (ENOUGH)

Active involvement should be enjoyable, driven by the desire among other things to make a positive difference, to have advanced knowledge and insight into the initiative and to be able to shape the future, or at least a small part of it. Our tasks as leaders are to maintain interest and motivation, to be inclusive, to promote and respond to questions. We have to balance the enjoyment with the serious business of the business. We can't let the buzz flip into full-on reverie. There will be a time to celebrate, but it shouldn't become permanent or it's rendered meaningless. As with so many aspects of the initiative, as leaders we have to maintain balance.

PERPETUAL INVOLVEMENT

Just as we've mobilized active involvement in the initiative, so at a point in time we have to begin to demobilize. The more successful we've been in galvanizing participation, the tougher the job will be of standing it down. Those involved will be asked to return to their day jobs. However, the challenge is also the opportunity.

At the point our initiative nears its defined conclusion, we need to consider how we maintain the momentum, and instil the spirit and practice of perpetual beta into the change we've created. Those who've been involved are our most important resource in this regard. We need not to stand them down, therefore, but retain them with specific reflection points and gatherings. As they helped create the outcome, we need them to stay associated. They had a special place in the initiative, they now have a special place within the alumni.

It becomes difficult as we're diverted to other activities and possibly new initiatives to devote time and attention to it, but it's essential. We therefore need to create a path with interventions, reasons to evaluate and return to the group. If we don't, the people and energy that got us to the vision will disperse altogether. It needn't be onerous or demanding on time, either for ourselves or our colleagues. A soft thread is enough.

The change never ends, even as it becomes something else. Involvement shouldn't either.

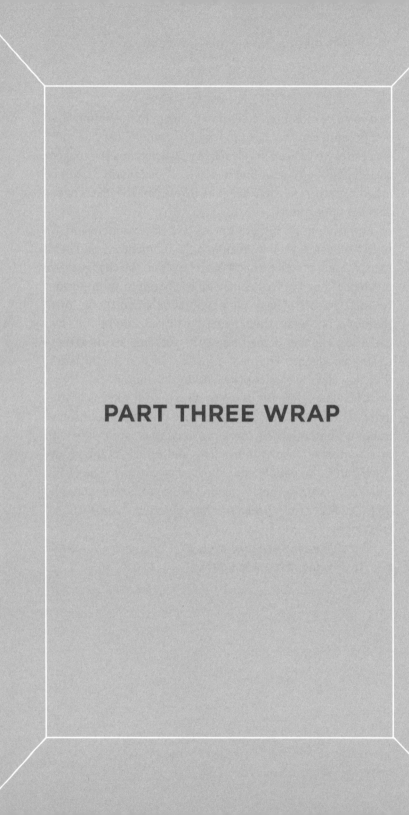

PART THREE WRAP

Here are a few points to reflect on:

- Importance is relative. To us, the small stuff can be everything.
- Change begins with the first words. We need to make them different.
- If we can't say 'stuff,' we're not there yet.
- If we ever think we're being clear, we're not being clear enough. We must always be clearer.
- If we feel like doing something, we're more likely to listen. If we feel like listening, we're more likely to do something.
- Negative emotions are an indicator of engagement. We have to work with them, not drive them out.
- An experiment can happily fail. A pilot shouldn't.
- We got involved for the wrong reasons. They turned into the right reasons – *because* we were involved.
- When it's all done, we may still not have thought it was a good idea. But we'll be there.
- If we wait until we've built the wooden horse it may all be over by then - release the Trojan mice.

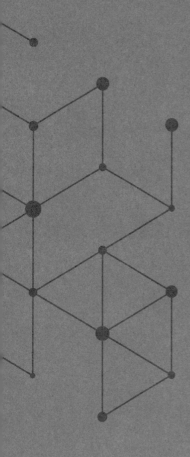

CLOSE

TINY SILENCE

We've reached the point we thought, on so many occasions, would never arrive. We're in one piece. Mostly.

We understood what change means and why we were changing. We prepared ourselves for how to make change happen using the operating system. We made change happen using the nine elements. We got stuff done while nothing stood still.

We have proof it happened. We can see all those affected by our change initiative doing things differently and talking about doing things differently. We had always been one of those people, but now it feels very different. We have some stories to tell, and we're ready to tell them.

Yet we shouldn't underestimate the emotional collision at the declared end of a change initiative. We're going to experience it, just after the tiny silence in which we draw breath.

We'll feel the excitement of having finished and achieved what we set out to with the fear of knowing that this is the moment of judgment in all its forms: relief that we can finally step off the conveyor belt that's been heading toward the clifftop; pride in our team and their togetherness and commitment and loyalty; disappointment for all the risks we didn't mitigate and opportunities we missed and curve balls that caught us square on; vulnerability for all the things outside our control; and regret that, despite wanting it to be over, the initiative as we understood and defined it is finally complete.

What on earth will we do tomorrow?

The tangle is proof we believed in what we were doing and cared enough to make it happen when there would have been numerous chances to walk away.

Then, we'll draw a longer breath.

We'll celebrate. All that emotion needs an outlet. It's easy to get sucked straight into the necessary tweaks and readjustments and the ever-changing flow we call 'day-to-day' that we've side-lined while the initiative was completed.

A formal declaration of the end of the initiative and an event to mark it allows everyone to draw their own line. Our colleagues need to feel like it's finished, so we can declare a date and say it has, whatever is planned for or happens the day after.

We shouldn't deny ourselves any of it.

REFLECTIONS

In the aftermath of our effort we'll be reflecting out of all proportion on the stuff that didn't go our way. There will be some. Optimism without reflection is self-delusion, after all. Chances are there will have been some setbacks, and there will still be some among us who haven't changed despite everything we did.

SETBACKS

Some things won't have gone to plan. Some things will have arisen despite the plan. Some things will have had consequences the plan didn't envisage. It's vital we're not unbalanced by setbacks personally, emotionally or practically. While earlier we tried to establish that some things won't turn out the way we envisage or hope (or others expect, however unreasonably in retrospect) no amount of placating will prevent us from disproportionally focusing on them. We'll reach for 'if only' with an uncomfortable regularity and ease.

Publicly we'll pretend we're not going through this. We'll get caught up in the modern trend for calling cock-ups 'learning' – a semantic trick to get away with publishing an amazing career-catapulting case study and avoid talking about the inevitable dark side – and ruminating on what we'd have done differently. As a matter of logic and physics, a preposterous exercise.

The route I'm going to recommend is in keeping with the aim of honesty and openness I've tried to portray through this book. Call them what they are, call them out, categorize them if there are many, recognize and acknowledge the particular context in which they occurred, explore with the team if there's anything that can help in future, and put them away where we know we can find them if needed. It's a cathartic process. It'll avoid the tendency to dwell on what didn't go our way. We don't want the angst or resentment sitting in our gut, eating away at it. The next situation will be just as unique.

In doing so we're also reinforcing a wider elementally safe environment by focusing on our vulnerability and humanity. Honesty and humility are incredibly endearing, and we're demonstrating the behaviour we'd like to see in others. We're in fact forming and working another change initiative.

As we do so, there will be those in our midst who haven't yet adapted, consciously or unconsciously.

OUTLIERS

In the bell curve so often associated with adaptation, they'll be camped out at the back end, either dug in and overtly declaring their opposition or passively just not engaging at all, even at the point we declare it's over.

As with the setbacks, there's a temptation to overly focus time and energy on the stubborn. There's a point of principle at play in our mind. After all the effort commitment, energy and focus deployed to make the change logically, emotionally and practically easy for them, they still reject it. We consider them anything on a scale from selfish to objectionable and begin to plot strategies to move them. Really, we mustn't. Negative energy is a sinkhole.

All outliers aren't equal. Adaptation for some takes more time. They need to see others doing things differently and hear them talking about doing things differently. They need the environment around them to evolve to render the old ways untenable or impossible. Those who made a noise about not doing so will quietly adapt as the spotlight turns away. It needs the shadow. Those who were silent, we'll barely notice change. Just like my colleague at the start of this book.

Evolution is also not inclusive or universal. Some will simply fail to adapt and will move away. Losing colleagues unwilling or unprepared to change despite the effort is a natural occurrence, not a failure. Let them go and wish them well.

They'll find an environment more suited to their world view and character, and likely be successful.

In categorizing the small minority of outliers, we're probably giving the out-and-out disruptors too much credit. But the benefit of the doubt is a decent thing. We can gift it.

KEEPING BETA BETA

Planning for 'day two' is as vital as planning for day one. In many respects, it's even more difficult. Day one isn't the end of anything other than day one, whatever we manage to achieve. Day two has no relevance at all unless we achieve our day one target. Thereafter, entropy will be at work, mixed with the euphoria and exhaustion of having achieved what we set out to. Sports teams, in particular, when having achieved their goal, find sustaining success incredibly difficult. Their personnel, ethos and culture evolve amid a landscape in which, as the incumbents, the toppling of their status becomes the prize. In our world, we simply want to ensure that everything we were successful in creating lives and grows.

Day two demands two things, as we shall consider below. As a backdrop, it's important to allow our initiative time to settle, for adaptation to occur, for evolution to unfold. Evidence is usually at this early stage anecdotal and therefore inherently unreliable. Yet there's often an impatience driven by an institutionalized need to prove the ROI, or executive positioning ("I told you it would work"), which should be constructively resisted. Of course, organizational politics suggests we can't always, so we need to be ready before the initiative is complete.

A RECAP

In Part One, we covered the idea of perpetual beta, which comprises three mutually supportive elements. First, viability. Our initiative doesn't need to be working 100%, as long as it's working well enough to deploy and use. Second, co-creation. We maintain an effective open channel of dialogue with the consumers or recipients of our initiative to enable its continued development. We enhance its viability while being aware that the external environment is also changing and therefore the expectations on its capabilities and performance may change, too.

Third, evolution. Based on the first two elements, the understanding that our initiative will never be complete and is always becoming something else.

Perpetual beta is therefore both a mindset and a practical process.

As a **mindset** it's about the manner in which we view what has been created through our initiative. That means seeing it as a collectively driven, ever-improving work in progress that helps us understand how it came into being, the path we've taken, why things happened the way they did (or didn't), and where it might go from here, complete with opportunities and risks. When many around us appear to see every initiative in terms of create, complete and depart, we mustn't be dissuaded. It's a mindset that will benefit change in our professional and personal lives. Hopefully, it will transmit to those in our midst.

On a **practical** level, it means we're effectively reviewing, appraising, adjusting and refining from the moment we've begun. It's natural and embedded continual assessment. The sort of thing we'd all rather have in our jobs than an annual appraisal (but we still seem to have annual appraisals). It simply occurs.

It also means that while we may have declared the end of the initiative, disbanded the team, wrapped the final accounts, gone out for lunch and got home after the trains stopped running, the change we created will need to be both informally and formally revisited for an indeterminate period of time, or until such a juncture where it becomes something else entirely. That means keeping some formal elements of the structure of the initiative alive and resources available, as we covered in Part Three. It'll need a revised brief for a given period or until they're required for another initiative.

REVIEW

That said, a formal assessment of the change initiative is almost inescapable, even if as a team we know what worked, what didn't and what might have been done that wasn't foreseen or thought necessary at the time. Time, money and energy have been granted to the initiative, and organizations need to know that the investment was worthwhile.

This book isn't going to dwell extensively on evaluation methods and techniques. That's probably another book in itself. However, we can look at this briefly for the purpose of awareness.

We're essentially back to the evidence-gathering process outlined in Part Two.

Quantitative data will be specific to the initiative, but still reliant for its usefulness on asking the right questions. To assist, technology may have advanced in this regard.

Qualitative data can be gathered through three methods:

- A **survey** has many advantages favoured by organizations – speed, ease and cost being some – particularly given the proliferation of free online tools. While they appear straightforward to conduct, they require skill and experience to deploy properly. This is especially so in regard to the framing of the questions.
- **Focus groups** or **interviews** have none of the advantages of a survey (in fact, the opposite) yet potentially provide far richer insight.
- **Open channels**, such as an Enterprise Social Network, offer real-time feedback and an opportunity on the part of the leadership team for clarification and further enquiry. They also usually have a polling function for spot survey questions.

A brief comparison is shown in Table 12:

	SURVEYS	INTERVIEWS	OPEN CHANNELS
INSIGHT	Broad but lacking in depth and nuance	Deep but lacking in breadth	Variable, dependent on take-up
SPEED	High	Low	High
PRACTICALITY	High	Low	High
COST	Low (online deployment)	High (staff and time)	Low (already in use)
COVERAGE	Potentially broad but rarely >50%	Limited to small number of participants	Potentially broad but usually dominated by a few participants
ANONYMITY	High (albeit respondents may still suspect that this isn't the case)	None	None (ESN rarely allow anonymity)
BIAS RISK	High	Moderate	Moderate – potential for 'bubbles' to arise
"SO WHAT?" POTENTIAL	High	Low	High
ANALYTICS	Simple – sophisticated, automated tools available	Difficult – requires specialists	Difficult, as only free text available – requires specialist thematic and sentiment analysis

TABLE 12

278

A combination of the three is optimal. Surveys can point to areas of potential interest that interviews and focus groups can explore in more depth. An open dialogue with those affected as adjustments are planned and implemented can refine the solution.

Very often a process and the tools associated are devised and implemented pre-initiative and repeated post-initiative in order to compare the results from each. The hope is, of course, that the initiative will have shown clear progress. It means the design of our 'pre' exercise has to be robust. It helps lay down a clear and early marker that we're going to hold ourselves to account. The weakness of this approach lies in its very essence. As 'everything flows' we can't meaningfully compare perspectives separated by the evolution that has taken place between two points in time. That said, it's a rather philosophical criticism of an approach that can, for the purposes of everyday organizational life, be overlooked. As such, it's worthwhile.

There are two cautionary notes, however. First, I'm a little sceptical of the adage "If we can't measure it, we can't manage it." It's important but it's not universal. It assumes we want to manage everything, the drive to certainty and control. I tend to think that if we can't measure it then it's probably quite interesting and should be explored. They're often the essentially human, emotional, unpredictable contributions. They are just as vital at this stage as they were earlier. We'll now have stories of the change and how it came to be.

Second, the data – objective and subjective, qualitative and quantitative – may well be the substance of another change initiative. Post-completion review is often a bridge rather than a conclusion. It's possible we're already on a new path.

PERPETUATION

Having set out their preferred process, many works on change devote significant attention to ensuring that change is 'fixed' or 'anchored.' The terms imply that without being somehow baked in the kiln, what we've accomplished is likely to be vulnerable. There are three problems with these generically similar terms.

First, in a world where nothing stands still, these acts are an impossibility. Our change is never finished. It's not optional, it's the reality. Everything flows.

Second, why would we even want to consider doing so? Why would we seek to prevent further development, enhancement and innovation, and stick with what we have? It's verging on the fearful, when we've shown no fear to get this far.

Finally, if we're introducing new ideas about change at this stage, we're lost. Everything we've covered will equip us for this initiative, and the next.

To keep beta beta, we need to deploy the same framework that underpinned successfully delivering the change. The adaptive, evolutionary approach described. Making stuff happen while nothing stands still ensures that what we have accomplished isn't unravelled. We just need to keep doing what we've been doing. We need to know where we are in our evolution, and be able to plan and prepare for the patches, minor tweaks and major adjustments to come. We've created a viable solution that will continue to adapt and evolve with the active help of our colleagues.

This entails facing in all directions, maintaining an awareness of the relevance of our change through open and effective dialogue with those for whom it was delivered, and with an eye on our developing universal, global and local influences. We need to ensure that the components of the operating system remain accessible, intact and functional. We need an emotional connection with what we've created, to instinctively feel when something needs attention. This means staying close. And we'll need a model for intervention – to inform, engage or involve, as and when needed.

The elemental framework isn't just intended for one-off, bookended activity. Embedded in a beta mindset it's open ended. Wherever we go, it goes. Yet leading the continued evolution of our initiative may not be our formal role any longer. As catalysts and creators, we may need to hand over to those more suited to steering its life to come. They'll need to understand where we've come from, how we arrived, and where we think it may be heading. We need to be available if needed. We're part of that alumni.

Open, prepared, dextrous, resourceful and optimistic: that's where we came in, several hundred pages ago. In addition to succeeding in its specific objectives, every change initiative should have a general aim to do some wider good. Ours will have presented a significant opportunity to shape the mindset of our colleagues as it relates to everything we encounter. It can open a channel to purposeful, sustained and effective change – from the why to the how and the what, and beyond. That's the most beneficial legacy we can ensure.

With great responsibility comes, well, more great responsibility. By this stage, we're completely fine with that.

THE LAST WORD,
FOR NOW

We have the same breakfast cereal we've had for a decade despite several repackaging efforts and a reduction in sugar. While we're eating it, we listen to the same news radio station even though the presenters come and go. We dress in the same clothing brands despite the challenge from unwelcome changes in our physiology – and we jog the same half-hour stretch of parkland to try and contain them, even though it's ever more crowded with others attempting the same. It was once a secret shared only with a knowing few. We head for the same stretch of coast every summer, despite its increasing commercialization. We book with the same taxi company for our transfer, even though the ride-hailing apps have moved in.

These may be patterns we recognize. We're okay with them.

Tomorrow is just like the day we started this book, only different. It's just like it because it's the end of something and the start of something. It's different because the river has moved on, everything around and related to it has changed. Including us. It's a world where nothing stands still.

So how do we get anything done?

We couldn't make change happen in a world where everything stands still. For us to move, other things have to move. Space has to emerge or be carved out. We work with the flow, not against it or in denial of it. As Confucius mulled, "The green reed which bends in the wind is stronger than the mighty oak which breaks in a storm."[114] We use all its energy and forward motion, recognizing the nuances and subtleties in how we approach it. We're primed for whatever it throws at us and we make change happen through ensuring our colleagues are informed, engaged and involved.

We've always been ready to lead change. We did a fantastic job and we're ready for another. As we've discovered, it's a natural response.

A part of tomorrow is already here and we're shaping it.

NOTES

OPENING GAMBIT

1. Tom Cheesewright, *High Frequency Change: Why We Feel Like Change Happens Faster Now, and What to Do About It* (London: LID Publishing, 2019).

2. Geoff Mulgan and Albert Bravo-Biosca, "Is Innovation Slowing Down? If So, What Can Be Done About It?" *Nesta*, https://www.nesta.org.uk/blog/innovation-slowing-down/ (accessed 29 December 2019).

3. Robert Louis Stevenson, *Virginibus Puerisque* (Tokyo: Hokuseido, 1925). The quote is based on a Taoist saying, "The journey is the reward."

4. Elisabeth Kübler-Ross, *On Death and Dying: What the Dying Have to Teach Doctors, Nurses, Clergy and Their Own Families*, 40th anniversary edn (Abingdon: Routledge, 2009).

5. "Kübler-Ross Model," *Wikipedia*, https://en.wikipedia.org/wiki/K%C3%BCbler-Ross_model (accessed 29 December 2019).

6. Friedrich Wilhelm Nietzsche, *Twilight of the Idols; and, The Anti-Christ*, trans. R.J. Hollingdale (Harmondsworth: Penguin, 1971).

7. Robert Matthews, "Who Really Discovered the Bell Curve?" *BBC Science Focus Magazine*, n.d., https://www.sciencefocus.com/science/who-really-discovered-the-bell-curve/ (accessed 29 December 2019).

8. For an assessment of the likely actual quote see: Daniel W. Graham, "Heraclitus," *Stanford Encyclopedia of Philosophy*, Stanford University, revised 3 September 2019, https://plato.stanford.edu/entries/heraclitus/ (accessed 29 December 2019).

9. Neil Usher, *The Elemental Workplace: The 12 Elements for Creating a Fantastic Workplace for Everyone* (London: LID Publishing, 2018).

10. Khurshed Dehnugara and Claire Genkai Breeze, *100 Mindsets of Challenger Leaders* (London: Relume, 2019).

11. Simon Sinek, *Start with Why: How Great Leaders Inspire Everyone to Take Action* (New York: Portfolio, 2009).

PART ONE: REFLECTION

12. Tim O'Reilly and John Battelle, "What is Web 2.0?" *O'Reilly*, https://www.oreilly.com/pub/a/web2/archive/what-is-web-20.html?page=4, 30 September 2005 (accessed 29 December 2019). The term is derived from (and also known as) the banana principle, as in, the product ripens with the customer. The originator of this term appears to be Peter Bosch in "If Language Technology is the Solution - What, Then, Is the Problem?" in Gerhard Heyer & Hans Haugeneder (eds.), *Language Engineering: Essays in Theory and Practice of Applied Natural Language Computing* (Wiesbaden: Vieweg, 1995): 225-230.

13. www.jarche.com (accessed 29 December 2019).

14. Luis is a digital workplace visionary who led the social technology initiatives at IBM for more than 17 years. He has been pioneering distributed work over the last two decades "encouraging organizations to work smarter, not necessarily harder" (his words when I asked how he would like to be described).

15. Edward N. Lorenz, "Deterministic Nonperiodic Flow," *Journal of the Atmospheric Sciences* 20, no. 2 (1963): 130–41.

16. "Henri Poincaré," *Wikipedia*, https://en.wikipedia.org/wiki/Henri_Poincar%C3%A9 (accessed 29 December 2019).

17. David J. Snowden and Mary E. Boone, "A Leader's Framework for Decision Making," *Harvard Business Review*, 7 December 2015, https://hbr.org/2007/11/a-leaders-framework-for-decision-making (accessed 29 December 2019).

18. David J. Snowden, "The Origins of Cynefin," *Cognitive Edge*, 24 August 2010, https://www.cognitive-edge.com/articles/summary-article-on-cynefin-origins/ (accessed 29 December 2019).

19. "There Are Known Knowns," *Wikipedia*, https://en.wikipedia.org/wiki/There_are_known_knowns (accessed 29 December 2019).

20. Slavoj Žižek, "What Rumsfeld Doesn't Know that He Knows About Abu Ghraib," *Lacan*, 21 May 2004, https://www.lacan.com/zizekrumsfeld.htm (accessed 29 December 2019).

21. Joseph Luft and Harrington Ingham, "The Johari window, a graphic model of interpersonal awareness," Proceedings of the Western Training Laboratory in Group Development (Los Angeles: University of California, Los Angeles, 1955). The Johari window is a tool for helping us better understand our relationship with our self and others.

22. Nietzsche, op. cit. (see n. 6).

23. Charles-Louis de Montesquieu, and Delphine Descaves, *Lettres Persanes* (Paris: Belin, 2019).

24. Herbert F. Barber, "Developing Strategic Lleadership: The US Army War College Experience," *Journal of Management Development,* 11(6) (1992): 4–12.

25. This quote is attributed to Sun Tzu, albeit there appears to be no direct reference.

26. In the TV series *The X-Files* created by Chris Carter (1993–2002, and again in 2016), the lead character Fox Mulder investigated unsolved cases involving paranormal phenomenon, including those associated with possible alien activity. He believed aliens were already with us.

27. Nigel Nicholson, "How Hardwired Is Human Behavior?" *Harvard Business Review,* 1 August 2014, https://hbr.org/1998/07/how-hardwired-is-human-behavior (accessed 29 December 2019).

28. Eyal Ophir, Clifford Nass and Anthony D. Wagner, "Cognitive Control in Media Multitaskers," *Proceedings of the National Academy of Sciences,* 106, no. 37 (2009): 15583–7.

29. Richard Seymour, *The Twittering Machine* (London: Indigo, 2019).

30. Mark Eltringham, "The Scale of the Problem for Workplace Design," *Workplace Insight,* 11 July 2019, https://workplaceinsight.net/bugs-life-can-teach-us-building-workplace-design/ (accessed 29 December 2019).

31. "Square–Cube Law," *Wikipedia,* https://en.wikipedia.org/wiki/Square%E2%80%93cube_law (accessed 29 December 2019).

32. Hoàng Trọng Hùng, "Is Leadership Innate or Learned? Implications for Leadership Development," *Hue University Journal of Science: Economics and Development,* 113, no. 14 (2016): 65–72, http://jos.hueuni.edu.vn/index.php/TCKHDHH/article/view/2627 (accessed 29 December 2019).

33. Riyah Collins, "Red Robbo: The Man Behind 523 Car Factory Strikes," *BBC News,* 4 November 2017, https://www.bbc.com/news/uk-england-birmingham-41834559 (accessed 29 December 2019).

34. Ellie Violet Bramley, "Desire Paths: The Illicit Trails that Defy the Urban Planners," *The Guardian,* 5 October 2018, https://www.theguardian.com/cities/2018/oct/05/desire-paths-the-illicit-trails-that-defy-the-urban-planners (accessed 29 December 2019).

PART TWO: PREPARATION

35. In a development of some ideas from my first book *The Elemental Workplace* (see n. 9) in a similar format, a good friend of mine, Ian Ellison, insisted the model had a name – and so having pondered it for several days, he called it *Neil's Diamond*.

36. David Hoffeld, "Want to Know What Your Brain Does When It Hears a Question?" *Fast Company,* 21 February 2017, https://www.fastcompany.com/3068341/want-to-know-what-your-brain-does-when-it-hears-a-question (accessed 29 December 2019).

37. Daniel Kahneman, *Thinking, Fast and Slow* (New York: Farrar, Straus and Giroux, 2011).

38. Amy C. Edmondson, *Teaming to Innovate* (San Francisco: John Wiley, 2013).

39. "What is Evidence-Based Management?" CEBMa, n.d., https://www.cebma.org/a-definition-of-evidence-based-management/ (accessed 29 December 2019).

40. Hannah Devlin, "Earliest Known Cave Art by Modern Humans Found in Indonesia," *The Guardian,* December 11, 2019. https://www.theguardian.com/science/2019/dec/11/earliest-known-cave-art-by-modern-humans-found-in-indonesia (accessed 29 December 2019).

41. This isn't my statement – but unfortunately the source is unknown (if it's yours – thank you!)

42. *Historia Brittonum,* http://www.historiabrittonum.net/ (accessed 29 December 2019).

43. Bruce Davison, former Adjunct Associate Professor at Columbia University and co-founder and co-creator of the GoSpace artificial intelligence (AI) application.

44. Cheesewright, op. cit. (see n. 1).

45. A quote often attributed to Plato, but the source hasn't been discoverable.

46. "Lee Trevino Quotes," *The Golf Experience,* https://www.the-golf-experience.com/lee-trevino-quotes.html (accessed 29 December 2019).

47. Shawn Callahan, *Putting Stories to Work: Mastering Business Storytelling* (Melbourne, Australia: Pepperg Press, 2016).

48. The phrase "Like an angel cryin' on your tongue" was used in the 1987 television commercial for Fosters Lager, directed by John Marles at RSA Films with advertising agency BMP.

49. For a super narrative on self-organizing communities, see: Colin Ward, *Anarchy in Action* (London: Allen & Unwin, 1973).

50. "Evolve Your Organization," *Holacracy*, landing page, 2019, https://www.holacracy.org/ (accessed 29 December 2019).

51. Ricardo Semler, *The Seven-Day Weekend: Changing the Way Work Works* (New York: Portfolio, 2004).

52. Unfortunately, I can't trace who said this. If it was you, it's an interesting idea.

53. Located at *The Quotations Page*, http://www.quotationspage.com/quote/23675.html (accessed 29 December 2019), and several other quote websites but I've been unable to trace the original source, if such exists.

54. Simon Heath, "Twenty Five," *Murmuration*, 8 April 2014, https://workmusing.wordpress.com/2014/04/08/twenty-five/ (accessed 29 December 2019).

55. John P. Clark, *Max Stirner's Egoism* (London: Freedom Press, 1976).

56. Thomas Hobbes, *Leviathan* (Ware: Wordsworth Editions, 2014).

57. Jean-Jacques Rousseau, *Discourse on Inequality: On the Origin and Basis of Inequality Among Men* (Auckland: The Floating Press, 1910).

58. Carlton J. Snow, "Building Trust in the Workplace," *Hofstra Labor and Employment Law Journal*, 14, no. 2 (1997): article 3, http://scholarlycommons.law.hofstra.edu/hlelj/vol14/iss2/3 (accessed 29 December 2019).

59. Ernest Hemingway, *Ernest Hemingway Selected Letters: 1917–1961*, ed. Carlos Baker (New York: Ernest Hemingway Foundation, Inc., 1981), 805. In the letter to Dorothy Connable he was warning her about Charles Fenton, who spread misinformation about Hemingway's life. The above quote is immediately followed by, "But this man is not a person that works with that system."

60. Robert C. Solomon and Fernando Flores, *Building Trust: In Business, Politics, Relationships, and Life* (Oxford: Oxford University Press, 2001).

61. Frederick Winslow Taylor (1856–1915) was an engineer who was among the first to work toward efficiency in the workplace, and the originator of time-and-motion studies. https://www.britannica.com/biography/Frederick-W-Taylor (accessed 21 February 2020).

62. Robert F. Hurley, *The Decision to Trust: How Leaders Create High-Trust Organizations* (San Francisco: Jossey-Bass, 2011).

63. Charles Duhigg, "What Google Learned from Its Quest to Build the Perfect Team," *New York Times*, 25 February 2016, https://www.nytimes.com/2016/02/28/magazine/what-google-learned-from-its-quest-to-build-the-perfect-team.html (accessed 29 December 2019).

64. William A. Kahn, "Psychological Conditions of Personal Engagement and Disengagement at Work," *Academy of Management Journal*, 33, no. 4 (1990): 692–724.

65. Amy C. Edmondson, *The Fearless Organization: Creating Psychological Safety in the Workplace for Learning, Innovation, and Growth* (Hoboken, NJ: Wiley, 2019).

66. Joost Minnaar, "Psychological Safety: How Pioneers Create Engaged Workforces," *Corporate Rebels*, 6 February 2020, https://corporate-rebels.com/psychological-safety-79185/ (accessed 29 December 2018).

67. Mark de Rond, *There Is an I in Team: What Elite Athletes and Coaches Really Know About High Performance* (Boston, MA: Harvard Business Review Press, 2012).

68. "9 Pairs of Teammates Who Hated Each Other ft. Man Utd, Liverpool & Arsenal," *Planet Football*, 29 March 2019, https://www.planetfootball.com/quick-reads/8-team-mates-hated-ft-man-utd-liverpool-arsenal/ (accessed 29 December 2019).

69. *The A-Team* was an American television programme created by Stephen Cannell and Frank Lupo, that ran on NBC from 1983 to 1987. The four highly likeable Special Forces soldiers, on the run from the authorities for a crime for which they were supposedly framed, always managed to extricate themselves from the scrapes they found themselves in by building something remarkable from scrap they found around them.

70. John Gribbin, *Deep Simplicity: Chaos, Complexity and the Emergence of Life* (London: Penguin Books, 2005).

71. Gemma Church, "The Maths Problem that Could Bring the World to a Halt," *BBC Future Now*, 9 June 2019, http://www.bbc.com/future/story/20190606-the-maths-problem-that-modern-life-depends-on (accessed 29 December 2019).

72. "Manifesto for Agile Software Development," *Agilemanifesto*, 2001, https://agilemanifesto.org/ (accessed 29 December 2019).

73. Friedrich Wilhelm Nietzsche, *Human, All Too Human: A Book for Free Spirits*, trans. R.J. Hollingdale (Cambridge: Cambridge University Press, 1996).

74. Marshall Goldsmith, *What Got You Here Won't Get You There* (London: Profile Books, 2008).

75. Carol Roth, "Why Henry Ford's Most Famous Quote Is Dead Wrong," *Entrepreneur Europe*, 13 March 2017, https://www.entrepreneur.com/article/290410 (accessed 29 December 2019).

PART THREE: ACTION

76. Brian Clark, "How to Use the 'Rule of Three' to Create Engaging Content," *Copyblogger*, 2 April 2019, https://copyblogger.com/rule-of-three/ (accessed 21 February 2020).

77. "Improv Your Biz," 2006–18, https://improvyourbiz.com/ (accessed 29 December 2019).

78. The Wise Old Elf is a leading character in the children's television programme *Ben & Holly's Little Kingdom*, created by Neville Astley and Mark Baker, and produced by Astley Baker Davies and Entertainment One (the companies responsible for *Peppa Pig*). It was originally broadcast on Nickelodeon in the UK. Elves don't do magic, but the fairies do and despite good intentions it never ends well. Magic is therefore best avoided in change initiatives.

79. Harry G. Frankfurt, "On Bullshit," California State University, Dominguez Hills, n.d., http://www2.csudh.edu/ccauthen/576f12/frankfurt__harry_-_on_bullshit.pdf (accessed 21 February 2020).

80. Carl T. Bergstrom and Jevin West, "Calling Bullshit 1.3: Brandolini's Bullshit Asymmetry Principle," *YouTube*, 15 April 2017, https://www.youtube.com/watch?v=-Mtmi8smpfo (accessed 21 February 2020).

81. Richard Carlson, *Don't Sweat the Small Stuff – and It's All Small Stuff: Simple Ways to Keep the Little Things from Taking Over Your Life* (London: Hodder & Stoughton, 1998).

82. The Pareto Principle holds that for many events 20% of your effort will produce 80% of the results. It was a phrase coined by management consultant Joseph M. Juran. He named it after the Italian economist Vilfredo Pareto who'd noted in 1898 that 80% of the wealth in Italy was in the hands (or possibly under the beds) of 20% of the population.

83. Shawn Callahan and David B. Drake, "Three Journeys: A Narrative Approach to Successful Organisational Change," January 2008, http://www.anecdote.com/pdfs/papers/Anecdote3JourneystoChange_v1s.pdf (accessed 21 February 2020).

84. Alex Lickerman, "The Importance of Tone: How We Often Communicate the Opposite of What We Intend," *Psychology Today*, 5 August 2010, https://www.psychologytoday.com/intl/blog/happiness-in-world/201008/the-importance-tone (accessed 21 February 2020).

85. Phillip Williams, "The Strange, Tangled History of the Acid House Smiley," *Red Bull*, 25 July 2019, https://www.redbull.com/gb-en/history-of-the-acid-house-smiley (accessed 21 February 2020).

86. Alex Hern, "Don't Know the Difference Between Emoji and Emoticons? Let Me Explain," *The Guardian*, 6 February 2015, https://www.theguardian.com/technology/2015/feb/06/difference-between-emoji-and-emoticons-explained (accessed 21 February 2020).

87. According to Wikipedia, the first recorded use of the smiley emoticon was by a Slovak notary of the 17th century, indicating he was happy with the state of the town accounts: https://en.wikipedia.org/wiki/Emoticon (accessed 21 February 2020).

88. "Emoji," *Wikipedia*, https://en.wikipedia.org/wiki/Emoji (accessed 21 February 2020).

89. This appears to date from a short article titled "Three Parts of a Sermon" republished on 13 August 1908 in the Hartlepool *Northern Daily Mail* (column 4 of page 3) from the *Sunday Strand* and is credited by the anonymous author to an unnamed veteran lay preacher. It's not an idea, as is sometimes thought, from Aristotle. https://www.britishnewspaperarchive.co.uk/viewer/bl/0000377/19080813/102/0003 (accessed 21 February 2020).

90. Arthur Plotnik, *The Elements of Expression: Putting Thoughts into Words*, 2nd edn (Berkeley, CA: Cleis Press, 2012).

91. Ibid.

92. "If I had more time, I would have written a shorter letter," *Quote Investigator*, n.d. The whole article deserves reading as it contains other similar relevant quotations on the benefits of – being economical. https://quoteinvestigator.com/2012/04/28/shorter-letter/ (accessed 29 December 2019).

93. Ryan Holiday, "One Sentence, One Paragraph, One Page," *The Creativity Post*, 22 July 2017, https://www.creativitypost.com/article/one_sentence_one_paragraph_one_page (accessed 21 February 2020).

94. Richard H. Thaler and Cass R. Sunstein, *Nudge: Improving Decisions About Health, Wealth, and Happiness* (New Haven, CT: Yale University Press, 2008).

95. Christopher Ingraham, "What's a Urinal Fly, and What Does It Have to with Winning a Nobel Prize?" [sic] *The Washington Post*, 9 October 2017, https://www.washingtonpost.com/news/wonk/wp/2017/10/09/whats-a-urinal-fly-and-what-does-it-have-to-with-winning-a-nobel-prize/ (accessed 29 December 2019).

96. Rachel Botsman and Roo Rogers, *What's Mine Is Yours: The Rise of Collaborative Consumption* (London: Harper Business, 2011).

97. Mark McKergow and Jenny Clarke, *Positive Approaches to Change: Applications of Solutions Focus and Appreciative Inquiry at Work* (Cheltenham: Solutions Books, 2005).

98. Kate Murphy, "It's Time to Tune In: Why Listening Is the Real Key to Communication," *The Guardian*, 25 January 2020, https://www.theguardian.com/lifeandstyle/2020/jan/25/its-time-to-tune-in-why-listening-is-the-real-key-to-communication (accessed 21 February 2020).

99. Charles Dickens, *All the Year Round, Volume XII* (London: Chapman & Hall, 1874).

100. Jean-Paul Sartre, *Nausea*, trans. Richard Howard (New York: New Directions, 2013).

101. Albert Schweitzer and William Larimer Mellon, *Brothers in Spirit: The Correspondence of Albert Schweitzer and William Larimer Mellon, Jr.*, trans. Jeannette Q. Byers (Syracuse, NY: Syracuse University Press, 1996).

102. Eric Hoffer, *The Passionate State of Mind and Other Aphorisms* (Titusville, NJ: Hopewell Publications, 2006).

103. Robert B. Cialdini, *Influence: The Psychology of Persuasion*, revised edn (New York: Collins, 2007).

104. David Robson, "The '3.5% Rule': How a Small Minority Can Change the World," *BBC Future*, 14 May 2019, https://www.bbc.com/future/article/20190513-it-only-takes-35-of-people-to-change-the-world (accessed 21 February 2020).

105. John Stepper, *Working Out Loud: For a Better Career and Life* (New York: Ikigai Press, 2015).

106. Robert H. Schaffer and Ronald N. Ashkenas, *Rapid Results! How 100-Day Projects Build the Capacity for Large-Scale Change* (San Francisco: Jossey-Bass, 2005).

107. Euan Semple, *Organizations Don't Tweet, People Do: A Managers Guide to the Social Web* (Chichester: Wiley, 2012).

108. "Safe to Fail Probes," *Cognitive Edge*, n.d., https://cognitive-edge.com/methods/safe-to-fail-probes/ (accessed 21 February 2020).

109. Dehnugara and Breeze, op. cit. (see n. 10).

110. Voltaire, *Candide*, trans. John Butt (Harmondsworth: Penguin, 1947).

111. Xun Kuang, *Xunzi, The Complete Text*, trans. Eric L. Hutton (Princeton: Princeton University Press, 2014).

112. Lisa Fithian, "Getting People Involved," *Organizing for Power, Organizing for Change*, n.d., https://organizingforpower.org/getting-people-involved/ (accessed 21 February 2020).

113. The phrase started out as "do cool stuff and talk about it on the internet" and is referenced on the *Community Lover's Guide* blog site where it mentions The Tuttle Club, a regular social media meet-up that Lloyd created, which was where we met. The phrase morphed over time into that quoted, to describe the learning style that Lloyd pursued. It's not to his knowledge written anywhere: http://www.communityloversguide.org/hand-made-1 (accessed 21 February 2020).

CLOSE

114. Peter Young, *Oak* (London: Reaktion Books, 2013).

ABOUT THE
AUTHOR

NEIL USHER

Neil Usher has wrestled with complex change problems for almost 40 years, solving them with a rare blend of straight-forward and creative thinking, together with an eye for both strategy and detail. He brings a wealth of client-side management and leadership experience from around the world in a variety of industries. He has been actively blogging about work for over a decade and his first book *The Elemental Workplace* was published in 2018. Neil is a sought-after conference and academic speaker, always bringing a fresh perspective while challenging assumptions and myths. That said, he prefers to be thought of as 'a regular bloke just trying to make sense of it all.' He lives in London with his family.